CW01329312

HANDICRAFTS OF RAJASTHAN

© Rupa Classic India Series 1998
First published 1998 by Rupa & Co.
7/16 Ansari Road, Daryaganj, New Delhi-110 002
Set in 9.6 on 11.5 Lydian Bt Italics.

Processed and Printed by R. N. Polyplast Pvt.Ltd.,
Noida-201301

ISBN 81-7167-377-5

Text: Mridul Bhasin
Design: Sagarmoy Paul

HANDICRAFTS OF RAJASTHAN

Photograph : Subhash Bhargava
Text : Mridul Bhasin

Rupa & Co

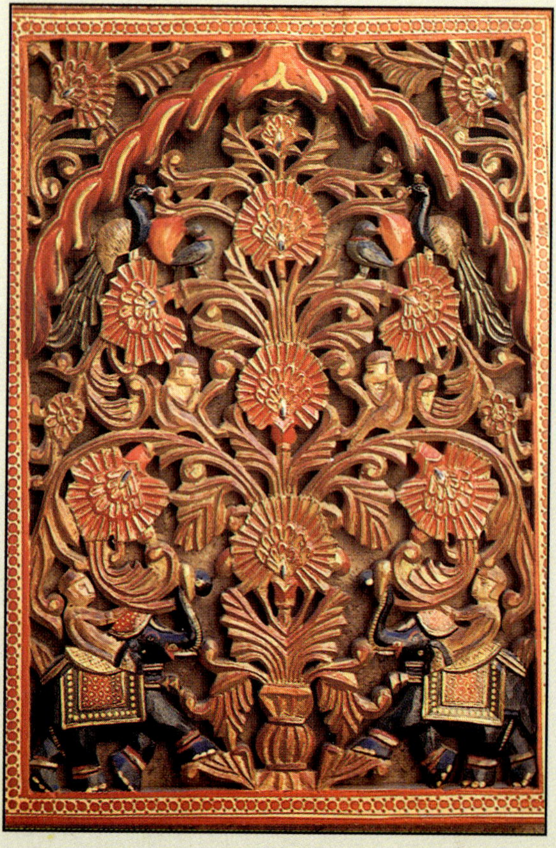

Introduction

The history of handicrafts in Rajasthan dates back to the Harappan Civilization, excavations of which in 'Kalibanga', village in Ganganagar district of Rajasthan, disclose the antiquity of crafts like terracotta pottery and printed textiles as they existed centuries back in this region. Handicrafts have remained a living tradition not only in Rajasthan but in every state of India. The craftsmen were bearers and perpetrators of soical norms wherein aesthetics, religion and life, all together formed a homogeneous whole.

Centuries old Indian tradition, social norms and human creativity were passed on from one generation of craftsmen to another to reach modern age, wherein today they stand as symbols of aesthetic humanism. The crafts of Rajasthan are, thus, an articulation of an eternal, human desire to reach out to something beyond material comforts. As a continuity over the ages, prehistoric rock drawings find their ultimate expressions in the hand-block vegetable prints of Bagru and Sanganer and the exquisite stone embellishments in marble. The leather embroidery done with finesse today in Jodhpur, the camel hyde gold painting of Ustas of Bikaner and the glass embroidery of Barmer, links ultimately with the primal creativity of people inhabiting the vast deserts of Rajasthan.

The division between a craftsman, and an artist was pointless in old times. The Sanskrit work 'Shilpi' as it was used in the various ancient treatise and later in the works of poets living in the courts of Rajputana envelopes skill, craftsmanship, designing and architectural art. The social status of craftsman became higher in ratio to his creative embellishments. Definitely crafts were not ornamental – they were a way of life. The artisans worked to fulfill certain ritualistic functions which spanned from birth to death. Pots, pans, paintings, images, games, clothes and furniture had a certain ritualistic value in a society where a religion played an important part in rural as well as urban life. The handicrafts and craftsmen were always well patronised in royal houses. After concretising their realms, the dynastic rulers of Jaipur had systematically worked to enhance the cultural aspects of Rajasthan by supporting indigenous arts and crafts as well as enriching them by bringing in artisans from outside. While the state of Mewar guarded the purity of Indian art and craft, the rulers of Jaipur encouraged cross cultural interaction in blue pottery, gold and silver jewellery making, brass work, stone carving and architecture. Today Rajasthan is not only the mecca of the exporter of hand-block vegetable-dye fabric, cut gem, jewellery, rugs, carved furniture and stone carvings, but is a must for the traveller too. Jaipur, Jodhpur, Jaisalmer, Udaipur and the Shekhawati region, lure the buyer, the traveller and the connoisseur to visit the region enriched with its royal romance and a colourful tradition in arts and crafts.

Clay pot in making. Clay crafts represent the earliest stirrings of creativity in man. The potter's wheel is perhaps the first machine made by man. Clay pots have ritualistic as well as utilitarian value in every day life.

8

Molela terracotta, Udaipur. Molela, a village near Udaipur has lent its name to this distinctive style of crafting terracotta figures. These consists mainly of deities of folk heroes and Ganesha.

Meenakari, i.e. enamelling on gold. It is done by goldsmiths called 'Chiteras' and 'Gharias'. Mostly Kundan setting is done in front and reverse surface has enamelling. Jaipur is famous for its fine enamelling.

Left: Meenakar Inder Singh at work.

11

Above:
Padmashri Kudrat Singh at work on a silver door.

Below:
Brass Patra door. The art entails making designs on a sheet of metal, brass or iron with chisel and hammer and nail it to the wooden surface in a pattern.

This delicate work, as it is done in Rajasthan, is mostly floral. Human or religious figures too are made in abundance.

Marble elephant. To perfect the artistically carved marble objects, artists also paint them with colours and gold.

A statue carved in the greystone of Dungarpur. Such artistic carvings have an age old tradition in Rajasthan where stone became a natural and frequent medium of artistic expression.

Chandan carving from Jaipur. This art flourished and survived under the royal patronage of Jaipur.

Painted wooden artefacts from Jodhpur and Bassi.
They are a continuation of a colourful traditional craft which expresses creative urges of a people living in the monotone of the desert. While Bassi's wooden objects use an admixture of lathe and hand crafting in making and colouring the objects, in Jodhpur the objects are mainly made by hand. The designs are the same as used in the miniature painting.

19

Wooden artefacts painted in gold.
Jodhpur, Kishangarh and Bikaner are centres of wooden painted artiefacts. Most Royal houses in Rajasthan have doors painted in lacquer colours with delicate designs on them. Amer fort in Jaipur has some exquisitely painted doors.

'Kavadi', – the mobile temples of Bassi, Jaipur.
The tradition represents the symbiosis of craft and religion which is still retained in the villages where the 'Kavadi' is carried from door to door.

Puppets of Rajasthan. The colourful, wooden, carved puppets are made in Rajasthan by the 'Bhat' community which is traditionally known as folk entertainers. Initially nomadic in character this community now dwells mainly in cities and still creates colourful puppets in wood and decorate them most imaginatively with scraps of cloth sewn together.

23

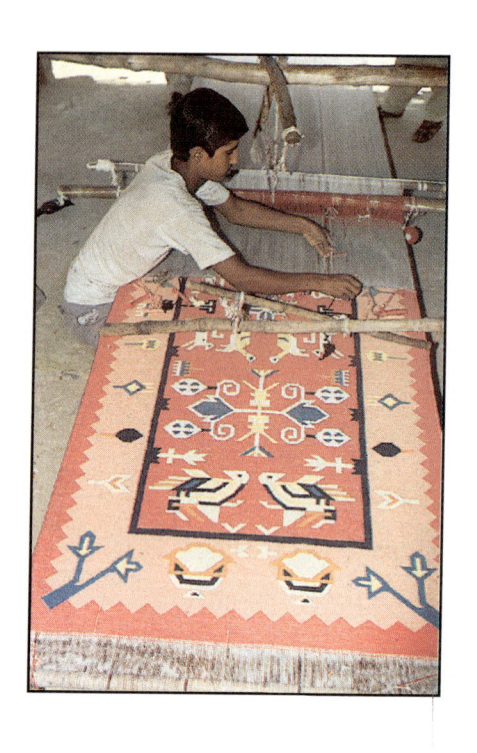

Durri from Jodhpur. Certain villages around Jodhpur consists of weavers only and Durri making is a home industry. While mostly simpler carpet designs are borrowed, sometimes designer Durries have mordern abstract patterns too.

Phad from Bhilwara. *'Phads' are cloth scrolls on which heroic tales of local deities or heroes are painted by a special set of people known as 'Joshis' attached to temples in Rajasthan.*

Phad from Bhilwara.
A certain community of 'Bhopas' still continues the age old tradition of singing the tales in villages using the scrolls as illustration.

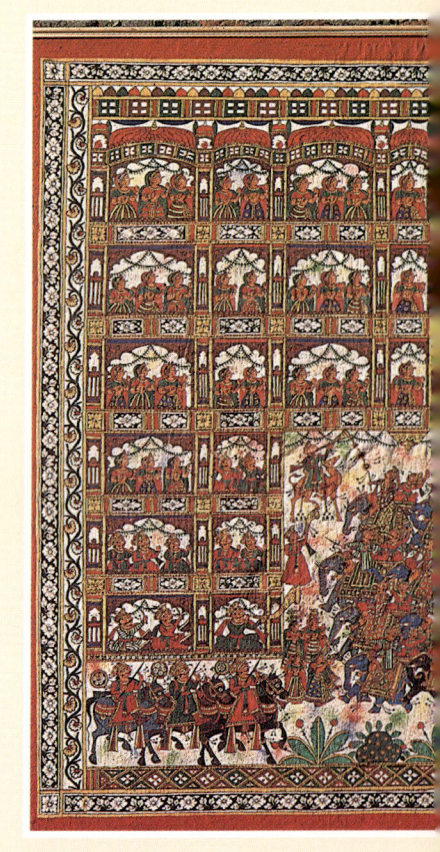

27

28

Left:
Painted Pottery. As pottery is also used on festivals, women decorate them with a variety of media.

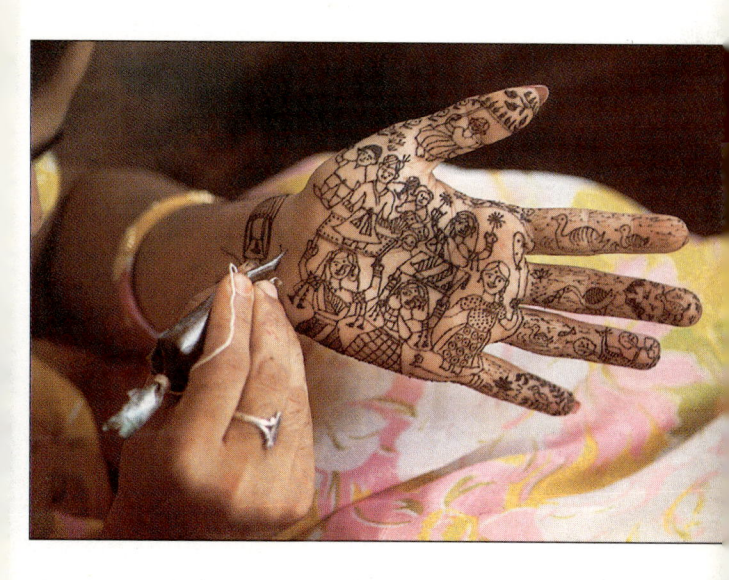

Above:
Mehendi. This herb is known for its cooling effect and colour. Various patterns are made on the palm on auspicious occasions. 'Sojat', a town in Rajasthan is famous for its Henna i.e Mehendi.

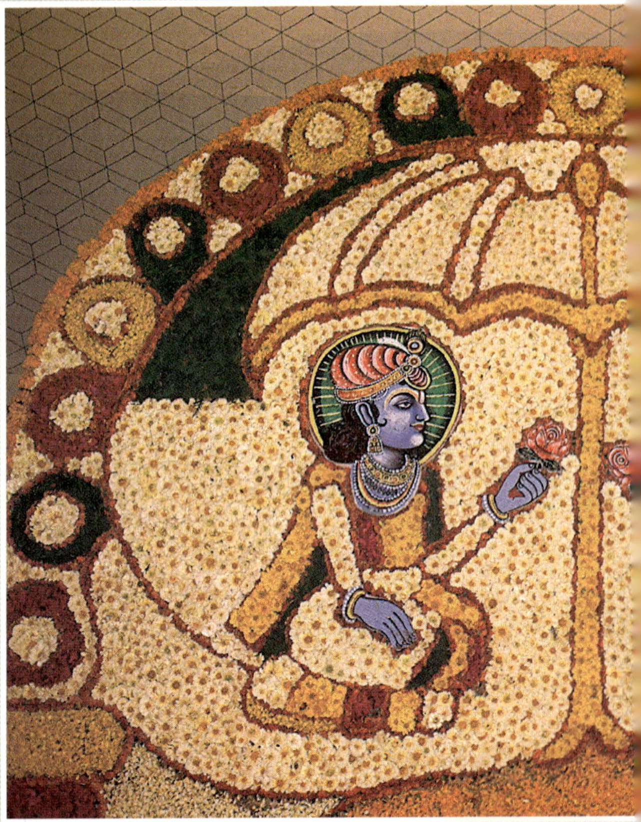

33

Marble Inlay. *Marble, which is available in abundance provides ample scope for colourful stone inlay on its white surface. Jaipur and Udaipur are famous for their marble inlay craftsmen.*

Tiles made of blue pottery. These tiles are still found intact with their turquoise blue and ultramarine in the havelis and palaces of Rajasthan.

Facing page: Gold work on camel hyde. *This work, as it is done in Bikaner by Ustas, is unique in its fine embellishment of the transparent camel hyde from which items of day to day use are crafted.*

Above: *Hizzamudin Usta, the master craftsman from Bikaner, at work on camel hyde. Colours and gold leaf work are used to enhance the beauty of the camel hyde.*

37

Aiwaz, the National Awardee for lacquer work uses his skill to create newer dimesions in lacquer.

Lacquer bangles. Bangles are worn by married women. In consonance with occasions there are different varieties of designs. Simpler lacquer ones embedded with glass are an auspicious sign for the married women. Couplets in Rajasthani language abound with descriptions of the 'Bindi' and the bangles.

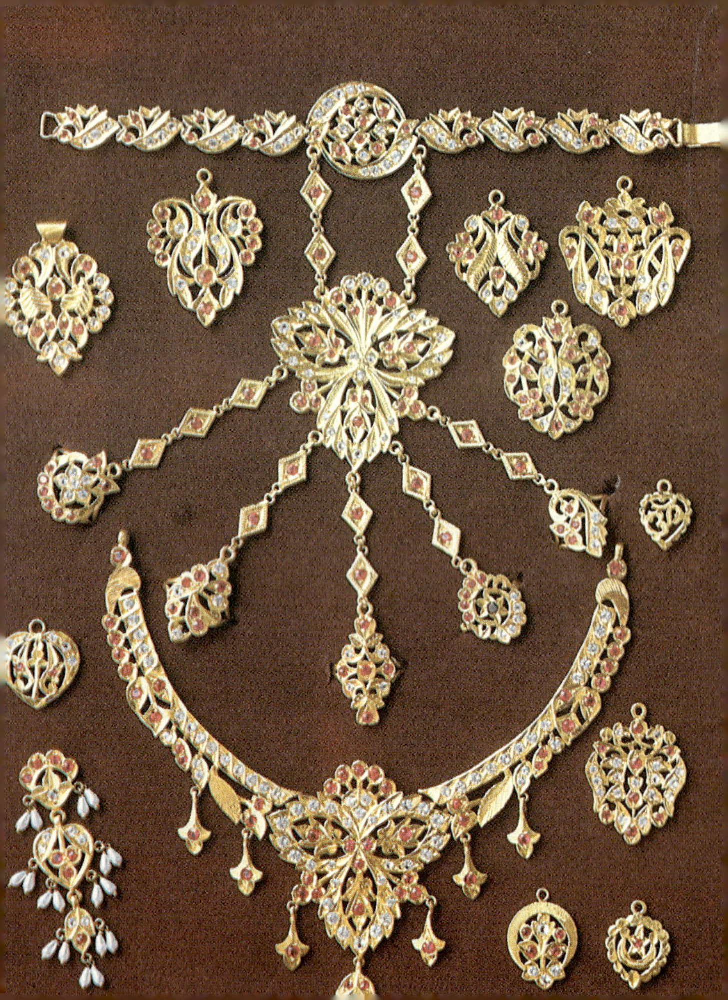

Left:
Silver jewellery. It is mainly the tribals who wear silver, gold being too expensive for them.

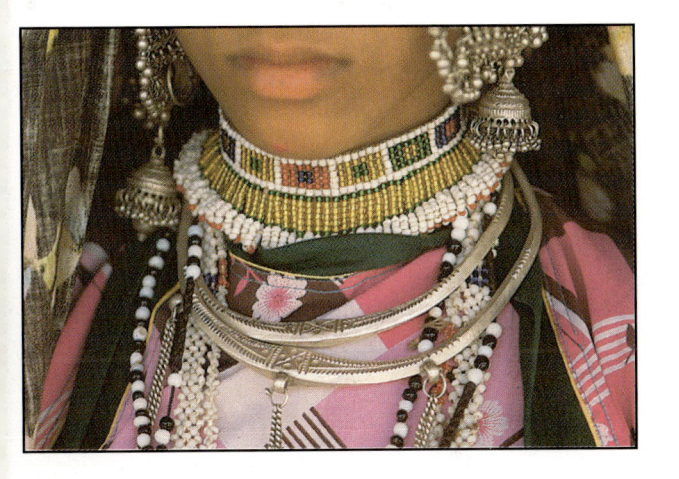

Above:
A 'Garasia' tribal women in her traditional silver jewellery. These age old jewellery items crafted by the villagesmith are in vogue today and have found a place of pride in jewellery boutiques.

Jewellery in lacquer. *Initially used only for bangles, lacquer is currently used for making all kinds of jewellery with enamelling and embedding done on them.*

Floral decoration for auspicious occasions like marriage etc. are frequently done by women of the house or commercial artists.

Miniature Painitngs. Rajasthan has various schools of miniature paintings. Artists working in Kishangarh, Mewar, or Nathdwara style of painting have successfully kept the art alive by handing it over from one generation to another. Legends of Krishna associated with Rajput history are the oft repeated themes besides 'Ragmala' and 'Baramasa'.

Tribal bangles. *Tribal jewellery in Rajasthan is made of metal with exquisite, intricate designing.*

Barmeri Embroidery. *This particular style of embroidery named after the desert town of Barmer is famous for its needle and glass work. The art is used for decorating clothes for wearing, wall hangings and various decorative covers for camels and bullocks too.*

44

Barmeri Embroidery. This craft is outstandingly beautiful in its manifestation virtually on every clothing used by the desert dwellers. Every girl in the household embroiders with cotton and silk threads using mirrors to create lovely designs.

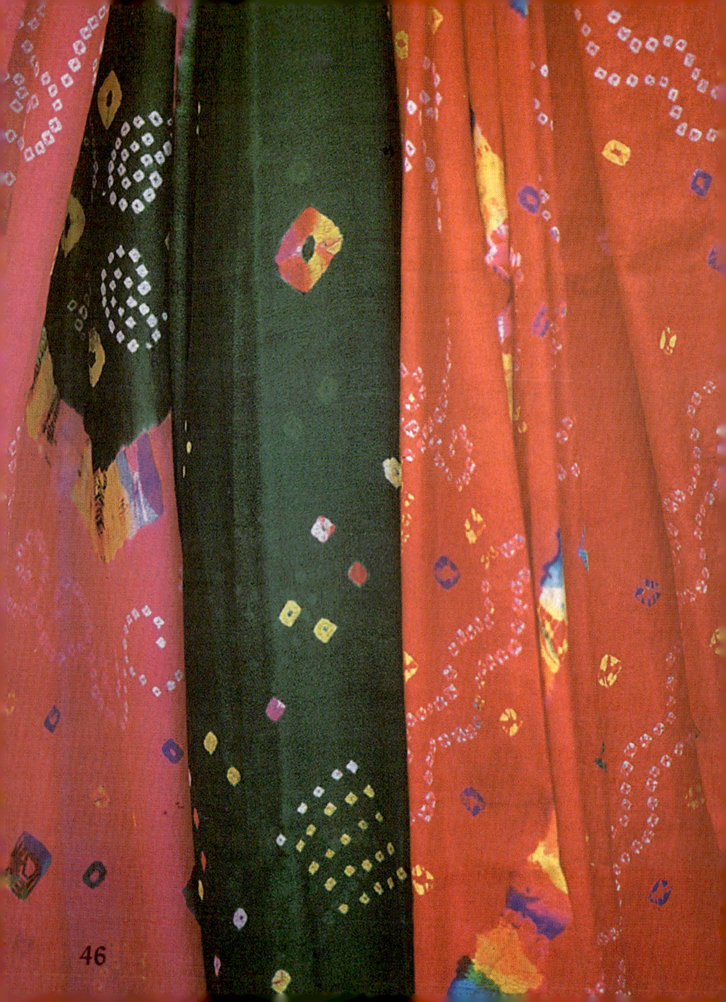

Bandhej. It is also known as 'tie and dye'. The colourful technique of fabric dying is prevalent in Jaipur and Jodhpur. The 'Neelgar Muslims' of the region have raised this craft to the level of a fine art.

Bandhej: Tie & Dye textile design of Rajasthan

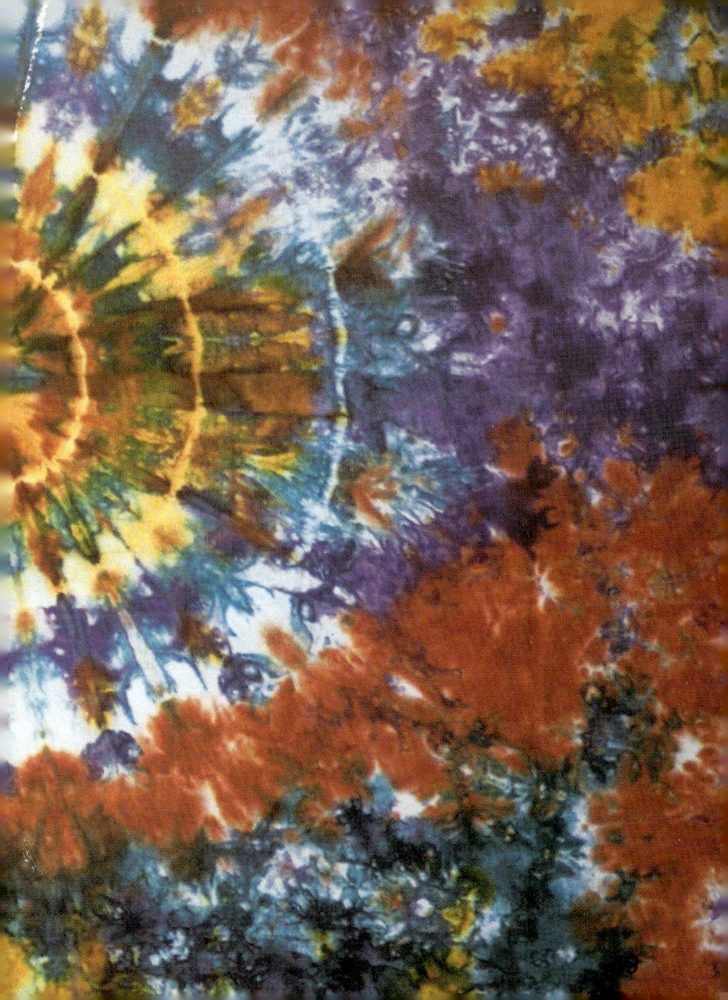

50

Bagru hand blocks for printing. *The artistic grooving on the wood is being done by a set of artisans in Bagru and Jaipur. These are pieces of art in themselves.*

51

Bagru hand-block printing.
The craft is eco-friendly in content as no chemical colours are used in this.

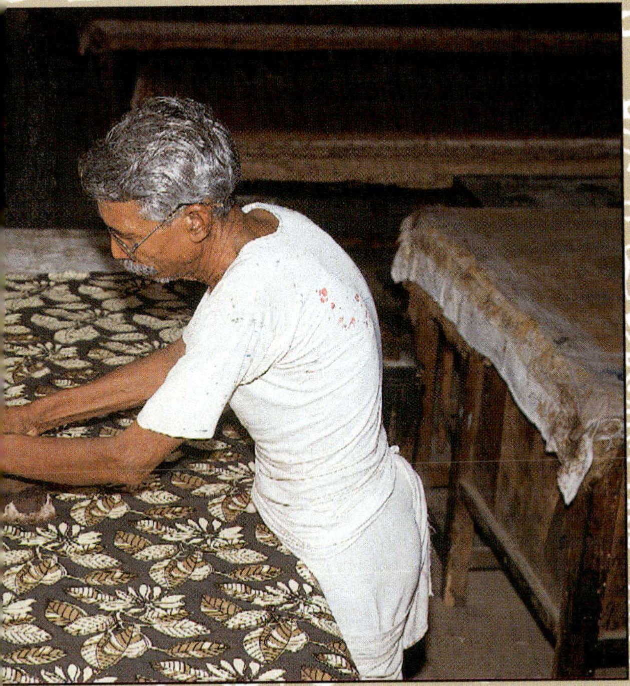

Below:
Brassware with coloured enamelling: In brass enamelling intricate engravings are made in profusion. Brass plates, fruit platters, Surahi lamps and animal figures are the most popular items.

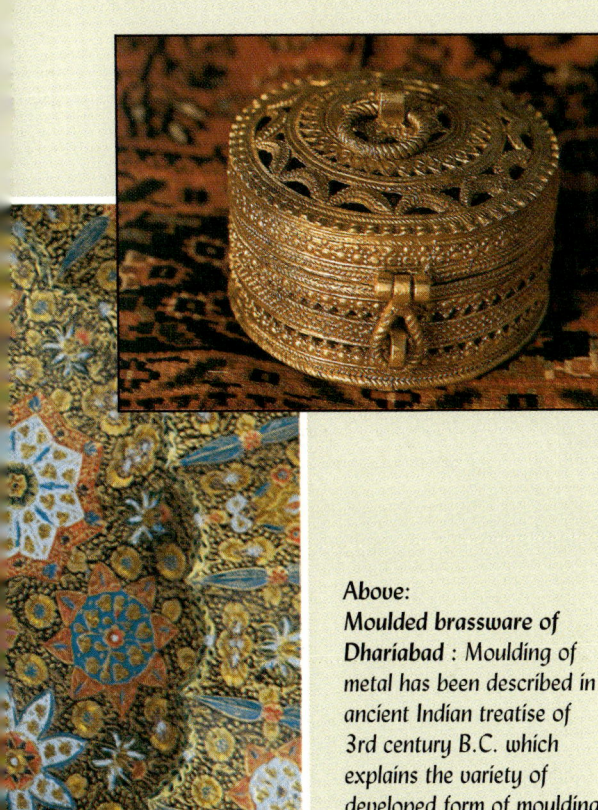

Above:
***Moulded brassware of Dhariabad** : Moulding of metal has been described in ancient Indian treatise of 3rd century B.C. which explains the variety of developed form of moulding in metal found all over India.*

55

Miniature painting.

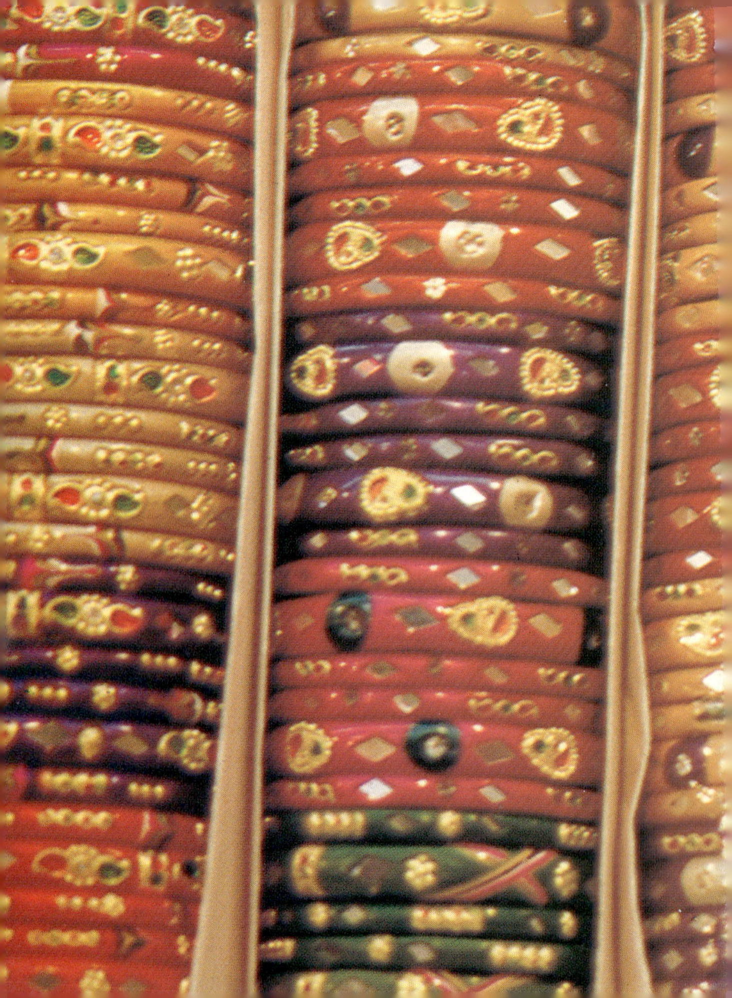

BERLIN U-BAHN ALBUM

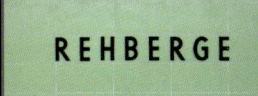

Berlin 2013

Robert Schwandl

BERLIN U-BAHN ALBUM

Alle Untergrund- und Hochbahnhöfe in Farbe
All Underground & Elevated Stations in Colour

Mein Dank für ihre Hilfe geht an Alexander Seefeldt, Felix Thoma, Hildegard Schweitzer-Thoma, Norbert Reulke, Jörg Häseler & Bernhard Kußmagk

Robert Schwandl Verlag
Hektorstraße 3
D-10711 Berlin

Tel.: +49 (0) 30 - 3759 1284
Fax: +49 (0) 30 - 3759 1285

www.robert-schwandl.de
books@robert-schwandl.de

2. Auflage, 2013

Alle Rechte vorbehalten
All rights reserved

Text & Fotos © Robert Schwandl
English Text: Robert Schwandl & Mark Davies

Druck: Ruksaldruck, Berlin

ISBN 978-3-936573-39-8

INHALT | *Contents*	
Einleitung | *Introduction*	4
U1	6
U2	16
U3	38
U4	50
U5	54
U6	74
U7	96
U8	126
U9	144
Bahnhofsübersicht | *Station Index*	158
Netzplan | *Network Map*	160

VORWORT

Das „Berlin U-Bahn Album" erschien erstmals im Jahr 2002 als erster Schritt, mich in dieser wunderbaren Stadt selbständig zu machen. Aus dem früheren Hobby wurde somit ein Beruf. Während ich andernorts oft gestalterisch sehr eintönige, standardisierte U-Bahnhöfe vorfand, faszinierte mich in Berlin seit dem ersten Besuch Mitte der 1980er Jahre die Vielfalt, die in den meisten Fällen die Entstehungszeit der einzelnen Stationen erahnen lässt. Die Erstausgabe dieses Buchs war also auch ein Versuch, mir selbst einen Überblick zu verschaffen, mittlerweile ist es zu einer Art Lexikon geworden, denn nirgends sonst sind alle Berliner U-Bahnhöfe in einem Werk so zusammengefasst worden.

Nun sind über zehn Jahre vergangen, ich habe zusammen mit anderen Autoren mittlerweile über 30 Bücher zum Thema „Städtischer Schienennahverkehr" veröffentlicht, und bei der Berliner U-Bahn hat sich einiges getan. Zahlreiche Stationen wurden in diesem Zeitraum modernisiert, manche wie auf der U5 komplett neu gestaltet, andere leicht verändert und z.B. durch Einbau eines Aufzugs den modernen Anforderungen angepasst, einzelne wiederum wurden im Zuge einer fälligen Sanierung sogar in ihren Ursprungszustand zurückversetzt. Deshalb war es an der Zeit, den derzeitigen Zustand aller Bahnhöfe wieder einmal festzuhalten, denn auch in Zukunft wird sich sicherlich wieder einiges verändern. Die knappen Texte beziehen sich neben wesentlichen Besonderheiten der einzelnen Stationen deshalb vor allem auf die in den letzten Jahren vorgenommenen Veränderungen. Die Bilder entstanden meist in den letzten Monaten und zeigen somit den aktuellen Zustand.

Berlin, im Mai 2013

Robert Schwandl

FOREWORD

The 'Berlin U-Bahn Album' was first published in 2002 when I was attempting to begin a new life in this wonderful city, and what had previously been just a hobby thus started turning into a profession. Whereas in other cities I had often found very monotonous, standardised underground stations, those in Berlin had fascinated me ever since I first visited the city in the mid-1980s, with their multitude of designs, generally giving a clear indication of when each station was built. The first edition of this book was therefore also intended to give myself a general overview of the network, and since its publication, it has become something like an anthology, because no other book has ever presented every U-Bahn station in Berlin in full colour.

Over ten years have passed now, and I have since published more than 30 books, written alone or with co-authors, on many urban rail systems, while much has changed on Berlin's U-Bahn network. Many stations have been modernised: some, like on line U5, were completely restyled, while others have only been upgraded slightly to meet modern requirements, e.g. by adding a lift; a few have even been restored to their original appearance. So it was about time to capture the current state of all the stations, because there will certainly be a lot of changes in the future, too. Besides giving the basic characteristics of each station, the short texts therefore focus on the changes made in recent years. Most of the photos were taken in the last few months and thus show the current status of each station.

Berlin, May 2013

Robert Schwandl

Einleitung

Das Berliner U-Bahn-Netz besteht aus neun Linien, die wie die Straßenbahn von der 1929 gegründeten BVG (Berliner Verkehrsbetriebe) betrieben werden. In den Hauptverkehrszeiten verkehrt die U-Bahn ins Zentrum von Charlottenburg alle 4-5 Minuten, abends alle 10 Minuten. Der Betrieb beginnt um ca. 4 Uhr und endet sonntags bis donnerstags um ca. 0:30 Uhr. An Wochenenden (Fr/Sa und Sa/So) wird auf allen Linien (außer U4) nachts ein durchgehender 15-Minuten-Takt angeboten.

U-Bahn-Geschichte

Die 1902 von Siemens & Halske errichtete *Berliner Hoch- und Untergrundbahn* verlief zwischen Warschauer Straße und Nollendorfplatz als Hochbahn, lediglich im nobleren Charlottenburg musste man von Anfang an unter die Erde.

Mit der Verlängerung vom Potsdamer Platz zum Spittelmarkt 1908 wurde auch das Stadtzentrum erreicht. Bereits 1906 war die U-Bahn ins Zentrum von Charlottenburg verlängert worden. 1910 kam die knapp 3 km lange „Schöneberger U-Bahn" (heute U4) und 1913 die Strecke der heutigen U3 durch Wilmersdorf sowie die Verlängerung durch die Innenstadt bis Schönhauser Allee hinzu, so dass bei Ausbruch des 1. Weltkriegs ein Netz von ca. 38 km zur Verfügung stand. Diese Strecken bilden heute das **Kleinprofilnetz** (U1–U4), d.h. das Tunnelprofil der fast durchweg in einfacher Tiefenlage gebauten Strecken erlaubt nur eine Wagenbreite von 2,30 m. Die Stromversorgung erfolgt über eine von oben bestrichene seitliche Stromschiene. Im Laufe der Jahrzehnte wurde das Kleinprofilnetz noch geringfügig auf heute 43 km erweitert.

Während das Kleinprofilnetz von der privaten Hochbahngesellschaft betrieben wurde, begann die Stadt Berlin 1912 mit dem Bau ihrer ersten eigenen Linie, der „Nordsüdbahn" (heute U6). 1913 fingen auch die Arbeiten an der sog. „GN-Bahn", der von der AEG initiierten Strecke von Gesundbrunnen nach Neukölln (heute U8), an. Beide Strecken waren der Anfang des **Großprofilnetzes**, das den Einsatz von 2,65 m breiten Fahrzeugen und eine von unten bestrichene Stromschiene vorsah. Wie bei den Kleinprofilstrecken beträgt die Spurweite 1435 mm. Nach den Verzögerungen durch den 1. Weltkrieg kam es in den 1920er Jahren zu einem wahrhaften U-Bahn-Bauboom, der den Berlinern neben der neuen „Nordsüdbahn" inklusive Abzweig nach Neukölln (heute Teil der U7) auch noch die ersten Abschnitte der heutigen U5 und U8 bescherte.

Nach 1930 gab es wegen der Wirtschaftskrise und des 2. Weltkriegs bis in die 1950er Jahre keine Netzerweiterungen. Nach einer Verlängerung der U6 nach Tegel folgte die neue Linie U9, die angesichts der faktischen Teilung der Stadt bereits als reine West-Berliner Linie konzipiert war. Ihre Inbetriebnahme erfolgte 1961 unmittelbar nach dem Bau der Berliner Mauer.

Die endgültige Teilung der Stadt hatte auch erhebliche Konsequenzen für das U-Bahn-Netz. Während die U1 am Bahnhof Schlesisches Tor gekappt und die U2 am Potsdamer Platz in zwei Linien geteilt wurde, verwandelten sich die Bahnhöfe der U6 (außer Friedrichstraße) und U8 auf Ost-Berliner Gebiet für fast 29 Jahre in Geisterbahnhöfe, die ohne Halt von den West-Berliner Zügen durchfahren wurden. Im Ostteil der Stadt verblieben lediglich die Strecken Mohrenstraße – Vinetastraße (heute U2) und Alexanderplatz – Friedrichsfelde (heute U5).

Berlin's U-Bahn system comprises nine lines, which like the city's tram network, are operated by the BVG (Berliner Verkehrsbetriebe), founded in 1929. During peak hours, the U-Bahn operates every 4-5 minutes, and in the evening, every 10 minutes. Services start at around 04:00 on weekdays, with the last trains running at around 00:30. At weekends (Fri/Sat and Sat/Sun), a continuous 15-minute night service is provided on every line except U4.

U-Bahn History

In 1902, the first route of the 'Berliner Hoch- und Untergrundbahn' [Berlin Elevated & Underground Railway] was opened. Built by Siemens & Halske, it ran elevated from Warschauer Straße to Nollendorfplatz, with only the stretch through the more affluent Charlottenburg being built below ground from the beginning.

*The extension from Potsdamer Platz to Spittelmarkt in 1908 took the U-Bahn into the city centre. In Charlottenburg, the U-Bahn had been extended into the centre of the then independent city in 1906. In 1910, the 3 km 'Schöneberg U-Bahn' (now U4) was added, followed in 1913 by today's U3 through Wilmersdorf, as well as a northern extension through the city centre to Schönhauser Allee. At the beginning of World War I, the network had a total length of 38 km. The original routes now form the **small-profile network** (U1-U4), i.e. their tunnels mostly run just below street level and are only large enough for 2.3 m wide trains. Power is collected from the top of a third rail. The small-profile network was later expanded until it reached its present length of 43 km.*

*While the small-profile lines were operated by a private company, the City of Berlin began to build its own line in 1912, the 'Nordsüdbahn' (the north-south line, now U6). In 1913, the construction of the so-called 'GN-Bahn' also started; this line was an AEG project that was to run from Gesundbrunnen to Neukölln (now U8). These two lines were the beginning of the **large-profile network**, which allowed the use of 2.65 m wide cars and introduced a third rail with power collected from the underside. Both small-profile and large-profile lines share the same standard 1435 mm track gauge. With World War I having interrupted the network's expansion, the 1920s saw a real construction boom, resulting in two more lines (the initial sections of today's lines U5 and U8), plus a branch off the north-south line to Neukölln (now part of line U7).*

From 1930 until the 1950s, U-Bahn expansion was halted by the economic depression and World War II. The extension of line U6 to Tegel was followed by the new U9, which was actually conceived as the first line exclusively for West Berlin. It opened in 1961, only a few weeks after the Berlin Wall had been erected.

The ultimate division of the city led to a number of important changes to the U-Bahn network. Line U1 was curtailed at Schlesisches Tor and line U2 was severed at Potsdamer Platz, resulting in two separate lines. All the stations on lines U6 (except Friedrichstraße) and U8 that were in East Berlin territory were turned into ghost stations for almost 29 years,

Introduction

In der geteilten Stadt entwickelte sich das U-Bahn-Netz sehr unterschiedlich. Während man im Osten auf den Ausbau der S-Bahn und der Straßenbahn setzte, wurde die Straßenbahn im Westen ganz stillgelegt und die von der DDR-Reichsbahn betriebene S-Bahn boykottiert, stattdessen wurde der U-Bahn-Bau vorangetrieben. So entstand in den 1960er und 1970er Jahren die neue Linie U7 (die heutigen Liniennummern lösten 1966 die früher benutzten Linienbuchstaben ab, das U wurde erst 1984 bei Übernahme der West-Berliner S-Bahn durch die BVG davorgesetzt), gleichzeitig wurde die U9 an beiden Enden verlängert. Nachdem die U7 im Jahr 1984 ihre heutige Länge erreicht hatte, wurde die U8 nach Norden erweitert. In Ost-Berlin hingegen wurde lediglich die Friedrichsfelder Linie (heute U5) 1973 um eine Station erweitert. Erst als die Kapazität der S-Bahn an ihre Grenzen gestoßen war, entschloss man sich, diese Linie oberirdisch zu den neuen Wohnsiedlungen in Hellersdorf zu verlängern.

Vier Monate nachdem die U5 ihren östlichen Endpunkt Hönow erreicht hatte, fiel am 9. November 1989 die Berliner Mauer. Während die Züge der U8 bereits zwei Tage später wieder am U-Bahnhof Jannowitzbrücke hielten, konnten alle übrigen Geisterstationen auf den Transitstrecken U6 und U8 bis Juli 1990 wieder geöffnet werden. Die Lückenschlüsse der durch die Mauer unterbrochenen Linien mussten noch einige Jahre warten: 1993 fuhr die U2 wieder durchgehend über Potsdamer Platz und seit 1995 überquert auch die U1 wieder die Oberbaumbrücke. Ansonsten lag in den 1990er Jahren der Schwerpunkt beim Wiederaufbau des S-Bahn-Netzes, bei der U-Bahn kamen lediglich kleine Ergänzungen hinzu, die vor allem einer besseren Gesamtnetzbildung dienten: 1994 Paracelsus-Bad – Wittenau, 1996 Leinestraße – Hermannstraße (beide U8) und 2000 Vinetastraße – Pankow (U2).

Der Beschluss, den Regierungssitz wieder von Bonn in die alte Hauptstadt zu verlegen, enthielt die Verlängerung der U5 zum Anschluss des neuen Regierungsviertels und des neuen Hauptbahnhofs. Dabei kam es immer wieder zu Verzögerungen, nur der Abschnitt durch das Regierungsviertel wurde im Zuge der anderen Bautätigkeiten mitgebaut. Seit 2009 wird nun der Abschnitt Hauptbahnhof – Brandenburger Tor als U55 betrieben. Das fehlende Teilstück bis Alexanderplatz soll nach heutigem Stand vor Ende des Jahrzehnts fertiggestellt werden. Andere einst geplante und durchaus sinnvolle Netzerweiterungen, wie die U8 ins Märkische Viertel oder die U9 nach Lankwitz bzw. zum Klinikum Steglitz, sind aus Geldmangel in weite Ferne gerückt. Des Weiteren wäre es notwendig, die U1 von Uhlandstraße bis mindestens Adenauerplatz und von Warschauer Straße bis Frankfurter Tor zu verlängern, ebenso wie die U3 von Krumme Lanke bis Mexikoplatz. Mit relativ wenig Aufwand würde sich so der Gesamtnetzeffekt wesentlich verbessern.

which West Berlin trains passed through without stopping. The eastern part of the city was left with just two U-Bahn lines, one from Mohrenstraße to Vinetastraße (now U2), and one from Alexanderplatz to Friedrichsfelde (now U5).

In the divided city, the development of the U-Bahn saw two different approaches: whereas in the East, emphasis was placed on the expansion of the S-Bahn and tram networks, in the West, the tram was totally abandoned, and the S-Bahn, operated by the East German Reichsbahn, was boycotted; instead, U-Bahn construction was given priority. The 1960s and 1970s thus saw the new line U7 (line numbers replaced the former line letters in 1966, although the U prefix only came into use in 1984 when the West Berlin S-Bahn was taken over by the BVG), while line U9 was extended at both ends. Once line U7 had reached its present length in 1984, line U8 was extended northwards. In East Berlin, the only change was the extension of the Friedrichsfelde line (U5) by one station in 1973. However, when the capacity of the S-Bahn had reached its limit, the new housing estates in Hellersdorf were eventually linked by a surface U-Bahn extension.

On 9 November 1989, four months after line U5 had been extended to Hönow, the Berlin Wall fell. While U8 trains started serving Jannowitzbrücke just two days later, and the remaining ghost stations on lines U6 and U8 had been reopened by July 1990, several years passed before the divided lines were reestablished: in 1993, line U2 began through-operation via Potsdamer Platz, and in 1995, line U1 once again started crossing the River Spree on the Oberbaumbrücke to reach Warschauer Straße. During the 1990s, however, priority was given to the reconstruction of the S-Bahn network, and only short extensions were built for the U-Bahn: in 1994, Paracelsus-Bad – Wittenau; in 1996, Leinestraße – Hermannstraße (both on line U8); and in 2000, Vinetastraße – Pankow (U2).

The decision to transfer the seat of the federal government from Bonn to Berlin included the extension of line U5 from Alexanderplatz to serve the new government district as well as the new central railway station. The project has suffered many delays, and as part of the overall infrastructure, only the section through the government district has been built. Since 2009, shuttle line U55 has been operating between Hauptbahnhof and Brandenburger Tor. The missing middle section between Brandenburger Tor and Alexanderplatz is currently predicted to be completed before the end of the decade. Other projects have been shelved, although some of them, like line U8 to Märkisches Viertel or line U9 to Lankwitz and Klinikum Steglitz, would certainly be useful. U1 extensions from Uhlandstraße to at least Adenauerplatz, as well as from Warschauer Straße to Frankfurter Tor, along with a U3 extension from Krumme Lanke to Mexikoplatz, would not require a large investment, but would improve the overall network layout considerably.

Erfahren Sie mehr über den städtischen Schienennahverkehr in Berlin in unserem Buch:

Learn more about Berlin's urban rail systems in our book:

U-BAHN, S-BAHN & TRAM IN BERLIN

von Robert Schwandl

ISBN 978-3-936573-32-9
(Text deutsch & *English*)

U1 Uhlandstraße – Warschauer Straße

Oberbaumbrücke (Schlesisches Tor > Warschauer Straße)

Auf ihrer heutigen Strecke verkehrt die U1 erst seit 2004. In der geteilten Stadt war die Strecke zur Warschauer Straße (ehem. Linie B) mit dem Ast nach Ruhleben und ab 1993 mit dem Ast nach Krumme Lanke als U1 verbunden.

Der als Hochbahn ausgeführte Abschnitt zwischen Gleisdreieck und Warschauer Straße gehört zu Berlins erster U-Bahn aus dem Jahr 1902. Der kurze Stummel bis zur Uhlandstraße kam 1913 als erster Abschnitt einer Kurfürstendammlinie hinzu, die jedoch bis heute nicht weitergebaut wurde, auch wenn dafür im Laufe der Jahre einige Vorleistungen erbracht wurden (z. B. am Adenauerplatz und Messedamm). Der mittlere Abschnitt zwischen Wittenbergplatz und Gleisdreieck wurde schließlich 1926 als Entlastungsstrecke für die heute von der U2 befahrene Hochbahnstrecke via Bülowstraße eröffnet.

Der Bau der Berliner Mauer bedeutete für diese Linie den Verlust der östlichen Endstation, die bis zum Wiederaufbau des Viadukts auf der Oberbaumbrücke 1995 vom Netz getrennt war.

Line U1 has only been running on its current route since 2004. In the divided city, the route to Warschauer Straße (formerly line B) used to be connected as U1 to the Ruhleben branch, and from 1993, to the Krumme Lanke branch.

The elevated section between Gleisdreieck and Warschauer Straße was part of Berlin's first metro line, which opened in 1902. The short stub to Uhlandstraße added in 1913 was intended to be the first section of the Kurfürstendamm line, which has never materialised, although some provisions have been made over the years (e.g. at Adenauerplatz and Messedamm). The middle section between Wittenbergplatz and Gleisdreieck was opened in 1926 as a relief route for the elevated section via Bülowstraße currently served by line U2.

With the erection of the Berlin Wall in 1961, the line lost its eastern terminus, which was only reconnected after the elevated structure on Oberbaumbrücke had been rebuilt in 1995.

U1

8.9 km (5.6 km oberirdisch | surface)
(0.8 km gemeinsam mit U3 | shared with U3)
13 Bahnhöfe | stations

18-02-1902 [Potsdamer Platz –] Möckernbrücke – Osthafen (Stralauer Thor)
17-08-1902 Osthafen – Warschauer Straße
03-11-1912 + Gleisdreieck
12-10-1913 Wittenbergplatz – Uhlandstraße
24-10-1926 Gleisdreieck – Wittenbergplatz (via Kurfürstenstraße)
1945 [X] Osthafen
02-09-1961 + Kurfürstendamm
13-08-1961 [X] Schlesisches Tor – Warschauer Straße
14-10-1995 Schlesisches Tor – Warschauer Straße*

[X] Schließung | Closure   * Wiederinbetriebnahme | Reopening

Der U-Bhf **Uhlandstraße** ist nun genau 100 Jahre westlicher Endpunkt der einst Richtung S-Bahnhof Halensee geplanten Kurfürstendammlinie. Der weitgehend original erhaltene Bahnhof erhielt 2005 einen zweiten Ausgang und 2010 einen Aufzug.

Von Mitte der 1960er Jahre bis 1993 pendelte die Linie 3 zwischen Uhlandstraße und Wittenbergplatz, danach wurden die Züge bis 2004 von Uhlandstraße als U15 parallel zur U1 bis Schlesisches Tor bzw. ab 1995 bis Warschauer Straße durchgebunden.

For exactly 100 years, **Uhlandstraße** has been the western end of what was once planned to become a longer Kurfürstendamm line. A second exit was added to this well-preserved station in 2005, and a lift was installed in 2010.

From the mid 1960s until 1993, line 3 shuttled between Uhlandstraße and Wittenbergplatz. After that and until 2004, trains from Uhlandstraße were labelled U15 and shared tracks with line U1 to Schlesisches Tor and from 1995 to Warschauer Straße

Hallesches Tor > Möckernbrücke

12-10-1913   **Uhlandstraße**   U1

U1 — Kurfürstendamm — 02-09-1961

▶ U9

Der U-Bhf **Kurfürstendamm** wurde 1961 im Zuge des Baus der U9 auf dem bestehenden Ast eingefügt. Die östlichen Zugänge befinden sich nur knapp 50 m von denen des U-Bhf Zoologischer Garten auf der U2. Seit 2012 ist der Bahnsteig in Richtung Uhlandstraße von der Oberfläche aus mit einem Aufzug erreichbar (unten), zur U9 kommt man von diesem Bahnsteig schon länger barrierefrei.

Im fünfgleisigen U-Bhf **Wittenbergplatz** hält die U1 Richtung Osten an einem eigenen Bahnsteig an der Südseite, Richtung Westen teilt sie sich die Bahnsteigkante mit der U3 Richtung Krumme Lanke, während man am selben Bahnsteig gegenüber in die U2 nach Ruhleben umsteigen kann.

Zwischen Wittenbergplatz und Nollendorfplatz fahren die U1 und die U3 auf denselben Gleisen. Am **Nollendorfplatz** halten sie Richtung Osten auf demselben Gleis auf der oberen Ebene des doppelstöckigen U-Bahnhofs. Richtung Westen steht den beiden Linien auf der unteren Ebene jeweils ein eigenes Gleis zur Verfügung.

Wittenbergplatz

Kurfürstendamm station was added to the existing branch in 1961 in conjunction with the construction of line U9. The eastern entrances are just 50 m from those leading to Zoologischer Garten station on line U2. Since 2012 the westbound platform has been accessible from the surface via a lift (left), with a second lift from this platform down to line U9 having already been available for some time.

The 5-track underground station **Wittenbergplatz** has a separate platform on the south side for eastbound U1 trains, while westbound trains share the track with U3 trains to Krumme Lanke, with cross-platform interchange available to U2 trains heading to Ruhleben.

Between Wittenbergplatz and Nollendorfplatz lines U1 and U3 run on the same tracks. At **Nollendorfplatz** eastbound trains stop on the same track on the upper level of the bi-level underground station, while in the westbound direction, a dedicated track is available for each line on the lower level.

11-03-1902 **Wittenbergplatz** **U1**

▶ U2 U3

24-10-1926 **Nollendorfplatz** **U1**

▶ U2 U3 U4

9

U1 Kurfürstenstraße 24-10-1926

Der U-Bhf **Kurfürstenstraße** liegt in einfacher Tiefenlage ohne Zwischengeschosse auf der 1926 eröffneten Entlastungsstrecke. Das farbenfrohe Muster an den Seitenwänden stammt von 1985. Kurz nach dieser Station steigt die Strecke an und geht in Hochlage, die Rampe in den Hinterhöfen zwischen Kurfürsten- und Pohlstraße ist jedoch bis kurz vor Gleisdreieck eingehaust.

Der Turmbahnhof **Gleisdreieck** entstand erst 1912 nach einem schweren Unfall anstelle eines tatsächlichen Gleisdreiecks, wo sich die drei Äste der ursprünglichen Hochbahn von 1902 trafen. Die vom Osten kommende Strecke wurde auf die obere Ebene eingeführt und endete hier dann bis 1926. Die gesamte Bahnhofsanlage mitsamt dem U2-Bahnsteig auf der unteren Ebene wird seit einigen Jahren saniert.

Der Hochbahnhof **Möckernbrücke** liegt direkt am Landwehrkanal. Fahrgäste, die zur U7 umsteigen, überqueren diesen auf einer eingehausten Brücke. Die Station, die ursprünglich der Station Görlitzer Bahnhof ähnelte, wurde bereits 1937 etwas weiter westlich neu errichtet.

Opened in 1926 on the so-called relief line, **Kurfürstenstraße** station lies just below street level without mezzanines. The colourful pattern on the side walls dates from 1985. Right after the station, the tracks climb onto an elevated structure, but the ramp through the backyards of the houses between Kurfürstenstraße and Pohlstraße is encased almost all the way to Gleisdreieck.

The bi-level **Gleisdreieck** station was built in 1912 following a fatal accident on what used to be a real triangular junction (German 'Gleisdreieck'), where the three legs of the original 1902 elevated line converged. The eastern route now enters the station on the upper level, where trains used to terminate until 1926. The entire station complex, including the U2 platform on the lower level, is currently being renovated.

The elevated **Möckernbrücke** station lies adjacent to the Landwehrkanal. Passengers transferring to line U7 cross this canal on an encased footbridge. This station, which used to be similar to Görlitzer Bahnhof, was relocated slightly further west in 1937.

03-11-1912 — **Gleisdreieck** — U1

▶ U2

18-02-1902 — **Möckernbrücke** — U1

▶ U7

11

U1 — Hallesches Tor — 18-02-1902

▶ U6

Der Bahnsteig Richtung Warschauer Straße des Hochbahnhofs **Hallesches Tor** schwebt über dem Landwehrkanal. Während der für Berlin relativ lange Umsteigetunnel zur U6 bereits 2012 neu gestaltet wurde, befindet sich der Übergangsbereich unter den U1-Bahnsteigen derzeit im Zuge eines Aufzugeinbaus im Umbau.

Am Hochbahnhof **Prinzenstraße** ist zwar die ursprüngliche einfache Bahnsteigüberdachung weitgehend erhalten, der an der Nordseite auch einst in ein benachbartes Gebäude integrierte Zugang sowie das an der Südseite freistehende Zugangsgebäude wurden jedoch 1984 bzw. 1991 neu gebaut.

Der ursprüngliche Hochbahnhof am **Kottbusser Tor**, der wie die anderen auf dieser Strecke Seitenbahnsteige aufwies, wurde bereits 1929 durch einen Neubau ersetzt, um das Umsteigen zur 1928 in Betrieb genommenen U8 zu erleichtern. Über ein unterirdisches Zwischengeschoss kommt man zu den Ausgängen am Platz selbst, während direkte Treppen an den beiden Bahnsteigenden in die Skalitzer Straße führen.

The eastbound platform at **Hallesches Tor** extends over the Landwehrkanal. While the rather long transfer tunnel towards line U6 was already refurbished in 2012, the entrance area under the U1 platforms is still under reconstruction, with a lift also being installed.

At the elevated **Prinzenstraße** station, the simple, though original platform roof has been preserved. The entrance on the north side, which had also originally been integrated into an adjacent building, as well as the free-standing access building on the south side, were rebuilt in 1984 and 1991, respectively.

The original elevated station at **Kottbusser Tor**, which like the other stations on the line had side platforms, was relocated in 1929 to facilitate transfers to line U8, which had opened in 1928. Via an underground mezzanine, passengers can reach the exits located directly at the square, while direct stairs at either end of the platform lead to Skalitzer Straße.

Hallesches Tor

18-02-1902 **Prinzenstraße** `U1`

18-02-1902 **Kottbusser Tor** `U1`

▶ `U8`

U1 — Görlitzer Bahnhof — 18-02-1902

Der Hochbahnhof **Görlitzer Bahnhof** vermittelt heute am besten das Flair des beginnenden 20. Jahrhunderts. Der namensgebende Fernbahnhof lag damals jedoch etwa 400 m entfernt, bis er schließlich 1951 außer Betrieb ging.

Während die übrigen Bahnhöfe entlang Berlins erster Hochbahnstrecke als Eisenkonstruktionen errichtet wurden, bekam der U-Bhf **Schlesisches Tor** einen eigenwilligen Ziegelbau, der bis heute weitgehend erhalten ist. Durch die nahe gelegene Sektorengrenze wurde dieser Bahnhof ab August 1961 zur östlichen Endstation der Linie B, später U1, bis schließlich im Oktober 1995 die Strecke über die Oberbaumbrücke wieder in Betrieb genommen werden konnte.

Direkt am Ostufer der Spree lag ursprünglich die Station Stralauer Thor (ab 1924 Osthafen), die wegen des kurzen Abstands zum Endbahnhof Warschauer Straße nach dem 2. Weltkrieg nicht wieder aufgebaut wurde. Der U-Bhf **Warschauer Straße** ist heute ein wichtiger Umsteigepunkt zur Straßenbahn sowie zur S-Bahn, zu der man allerdings einen kleinen Fußmarsch zurücklegen muss.

The elevated station **Görlitzer Bahnhof** best preserves the feeling of the early 20th century. The eponymous train station, however, lay about 400 m away and was abandoned in 1951.

Whereas the other stations along Berlin's first elevated metro line were built as iron structures, **Schlesisches Tor** was designed with an unconventional brick building, which is largely intact. Due to the nearby sector boundary, the station became the eastern terminus of line B (later U1) in August 1961. It remained in this role until October 1995, when the tracks on the Oberbaumbrücke were finally ready for service.

A station called Stralauer Thor (from 1924 Osthafen) used to lie directly on the east bank of the Spree River, but due to the short distance separating it from the terminus at Warschauer Straße, it was not rebuilt after World War II. **Warschauer Straße** is now a major transfer point between U-Bahn, tram and S-Bahn, although reaching the latter requires a short walk.

Schlesisches Tor

18-02-1902 — **Schlesisches Tor** — **U1**

17-08-1902 — **Warschauer Straße** — **U1**

U2 — Ruhleben – Pankow

Die U2 in ihrer heutigen Form existiert seit 1993, als der durchgehende Betrieb zwischen Mohrenstraße und Wittenbergplatz wieder aufgenommen werden konnte. Die Berliner Mauer hatte die alte Linie A 1961 genau am Potsdamer Platz in zwei Teile zerschnitten. Aufgrund der ausreichenden Kapazität auf der einst als „Entlastungslinie" gebauten Parallelstrecke (siehe U1) wurde 1972 der Betrieb auf dem Hochbahnabschnitt zwischen Wittenbergplatz und Gleisdreieck eingestellt.

Zur Strecke der U2 gehört ein Abschnitt von Berlins erster U-Bahn aus dem Jahr 1902, nämlich von Knie (heute Ernst-Reuter-Platz) bis Potsdamer Platz. Wenige Jahre später ging es weiter

Line U2 has existed in its present form since 1993, when through operation between Mohrenstraße and Wittenbergplatz was resumed. In 1961, the Berlin Wall had severed the old line A at Potsdamer Platz. As there was sufficient capacity on the parallel 'relief line' (see line U1), service on the elevated section between Wittenbergplatz and Gleisdreieck was discontinued in 1972.

Today's line U2 includes a section of Berlin's first metro line from 1902, the stretch from Knie (now Ernst-Reuter-Platz) to Potsdamer Platz. A few years later, the original line was extended west via Deutsche Oper to Wilhelmplatz (now

U2

20.7 km (6.2 km oberirdisch | surface)
29 Bahnhöfe | stations

18-02-1902: Potsdamer Platz [– Möckernbrücke]
11-03-1902: Potsdamer Platz – Zoologischer Garten
14-12-1902: Zoologischer Garten – Ernst-Reuter-Platz
14-05-1906: Ernst-Reuter-Platz – Deutsche Oper [– R.-Wagner-Platz]
29-03-1908: Deutsche Oper – Theodor-Heuss-Platz
01-10-1908: Potsdamer Platz – Spittelmarkt
03-12-1912: + Gleisdreieck
08-06-1913: Theodor-Heuss-Platz – Olympia-Stadion
01-07-1913: Spittelmarkt – Alexanderplatz
27-07-1913: Alexanderplatz – Schönhauser Allee
20-05-1922: + Neu-Westend
22-12-1929: Olympia-Stadion – Ruhleben
29-06-1930: Schönhauser Allee – Vinetastraße
13-08-1961: [X] Gleisdreieck – Mohrenstraße
31-12-1971: [X] Gleisdreieck – Nollendorfplatz
28-04-1978: + Bismarckstraße
13-11-1993: Wittenbergplatz – Mohrenstraße*
01-10-1998: + Mendelssohn-Bartholdy-Park
16-09-2000: Vinetastraße – Pankow

Theodor-Heuss-Platz

[X] Schließung | Closure   * Wiederinbetriebnahme | Reopening

Senefelderplatz > Eberswalder Straße

nach Westen über Deutsche Oper zum Wilhelmplatz (heute Richard-Wagner-Platz) und bald folgte ein Abzweig entlang der Bismarckstraße zum Reichskanzlerplatz (heute Theodor-Heuss-Platz), der jedoch die ersten Jahre nur als Shuttle-Linie betrieben wurde, da er noch durch dünn besiedeltes Gebiet führte.

In der Innenstadt wurde die einstige Linie A in mehreren Etappen bis zum S-Bahn-Nordring verlängert, bis sie schließlich 1930 Pankow (Vinetastraße) erreichte. Die Züge fuhren von dort lange abwechselnd nach Ruhleben und Krumme Lanke. Erst 70 Jahre später kam eine kurze Verlängerung bis zum S-Bhf Pankow hinzu, bis heute die einzige Verlängerung des Kleinprofilnetzes nach 1930.

Eine einst geplante Westverlängerung nach Spandau wird derzeit nicht mehr verfolgt, auch der Bau eines U-Bahnhofs im Zentrum von Pankow ist mittelfristig nicht zu erwarten.

Richard-Wagner-Platz). This was soon followed by a branch along Bismarckstraße to Reichskanzlerplatz (now Th.-Heuss-Pl.), although this was operated as a shuttle line for the first few years as it ran through what as then a sparsely populated area.

In the city centre, the old line A was extended in several stages to the S-Bahn's northern ring until it reached Pankow (Vinetastraße) in 1930. For several decades, trains ran from there alternately to Ruhleben and Krumme Lanke. 70 years later, a short extension was opened to bring line U2 to Pankow S-Bahn station, the only addition to the small-profile network since 1930.

A western extension once planned from Ruhleben to Spandau is no longer being pursued, and the construction of an U-Bahn station in the centre of Pankow is not very likely in the medium term either.

U2 — Ruhleben — 22-12-1929

In **Ruhleben** endet die U2 seit 1929 stumpf ohne Kehrgleise hinter dem Endbahnhof, der sich in Dammlage befindet und 2011 grundsaniert wurde. Ein Weiterbau Richtung Rathaus Spandau und ins Falkenhagener Feld wurde in den 1980er Jahren beim Bau der U7 noch berücksichtigt.

Bis 1922 wurde der U-Bhf **Olympia-Stadion** nur bei Veranstaltungen bedient. Das Bahnhofsgebäude von Alfred Grenander, in dem das U-Bahn-Museum beheimatet ist, stammt aus dem Jahr 1929, als die Anlage erweitert wurde. Die Aufzüge zu den beiden Mittelbahnsteigen (unten) wurden in Vorbereitung auf die Fußball-WM 2006 errichtet.

Der U-Bhf **Neu-Westend** wurde erst 1922 eröffnet, nachdem die Züge bereits seit 1913 zum Stadion-Bahnhof und vor allem zur Betriebswerkstatt Grunewald gefahren waren. Die Bahnsteighalle bekam ihr heutiges Aussehen 1986. Der östliche Zugang am Steubenplatz ist weitgehend original erhalten (rechts), der westliche kam 1936 hinzu und lehnt sich gestalterisch an den älteren an.

At **Ruhleben**, line U2 has terminated at a stub-end station without any reversing tracks beyond the terminus since 1929. It is located on an embankment and was renovated in 2011. An extension to Rathaus Spandau and Falkenhagener Feld was still planned for when line U7 was built in the 1980s.

Until 1922, **Olympia-Stadion** station was only served during special events. The entrance building by Alfred Grenander, which is home to the U-Bahn Museum, dates from 1929, when the station was expanded. The lifts to the two island platforms (left) were added in preparation for the 2006 FIFA World Cup.

Neu-Westend station was only opened in 1922, although trains had been running through to the stadium and the Grunewald workshops since 1913. The platform area received its present look in 1986. The eastern entrance at Steubenplatz has been preserved in almost its original state (above), while the western access was added in 1936, following the design of the older one.

08-06-1913 **Olympia-Stadion** **U2**

20-05-1922 **Neu-Westend** **U2**

U2 — Theodor-Heuss-Platz
29-03-1908

Am **Theodor-Heuss-Platz** endet derzeit außerhalb der Hauptverkehrszeiten jeder zweite Zug der U2. Die Eingangsportale am östlichen Ende sind aus der Anfangszeit erhalten, auch wenn die Zugänge in den letzten Jahren erneuert wurden. Die Westeingänge kamen zusammen mit zwei Aufzügen erst 2006/2007 hinzu (rechts). Die Seitenbahnsteige sind unterirdisch nicht miteinander verbunden.

Der U-Bhf **Kaiserdamm** wurde Mitte der 1920er Jahre im Zuge des Entstehens des nahen Messegeländes umgebaut, indem die Ausgänge von der Straßenmitte auf die Bürgersteige verlegt wurden. Im Westen entstand dabei ein großzügiges Zwischengeschoss, im Osten kam etwas später ein Tunnel unter den Gleisen hinzu.

Seit 1986 präsentiert sich der U-Bhf **Sophie-Charlotte-Platz** als kleines U-Bahn-Museum. Bis 2005 bzw. 2006, als die westlichen Ausgänge gebaut wurden (unten), war die Station nur von der Ostseite zugänglich. Die dortigen Ausgänge waren 1938 an den Straßenrand verlegt worden. Ein Tunnel unter den Gleisen verbindet die Seitenbahnsteige.

At present, **Theodor-Heuss-Platz** is the terminus for every other U2 train during off-peak hours. While the original entrance portals at the eastern end have been preserved, and were renovated in recent years, the two western entrances (above) as well as two lifts were only added in 2006 and 2007, respectively. The two side platforms are not connected underground.

Kaiserdamm station was rebuilt in the mid-1920s in conjunction with the establishment of the nearby exhibition centre, with the entrances having been relocated from the middle of the street to the pavements. At the western end, a spacious mezzanine was created, while at the eastern, a passenger tunnel under the tracks was added later.

Since 1986, **Sophie-Charlotte-Platz** station has appeared to be a small U-Bahn museum. Before 2005/2006, when the western exits were built (left), the station had only been accessible from the eastern side. Those exits had been moved to the pavements in 1938. A tunnel under the tracks connects the two side platforms.

| 29-03-1908 | **Kaiserdamm** | U2 |

| 29-03-1908 | **Sophie-Charlotte-Platz** | U2 |

U2 Bismarckstraße
28-04-1978

▶ U7

Bismarckstraße

Der U-Bhf **Bismarckstraße** wurde erst 1978 als Umsteigestation zur neuen U7 errichtet. Die Aluminiumverkleidung der Wände stammt aus dieser Zeit, während sich die Gestaltung der Stützwand zwischen den Gleisen sowie die Farbe der Decke und der Stützpfeiler seither mehrmals geändert hat.

Der U-Bhf **Deutsche Oper** wurde 1906 als viergleisiger Verzweigungsbahnhof eröffnet. Die Hauptstrecke führte anfangs zum Wilhelmplatz (heute Richard-Wagner-Platz). Dieser zuletzt von einer Linie 5 befahrene Abschnitt wurde 1970 im Zuge des Baus der U7 geschlossen. Nach einem Brand im Juli 2000 wurde die Station Deutsche Oper in ihr ursprüngliches Aussehen zurückversetzt, die sonst üblichen Werbeflächen zieren nun jedoch portugiesische Fliesenwandbilder. Ein östlicher Ausgang (unten) wurde 2006 errichtet.

Wenig Ursprüngliches ist im U-Bhf **Ernst-Reuter-Platz**, 1902 als „Knie" Endpunkt der ersten U-Bahn-Strecke, erhalten, da er in den 1950ern im Zuge der Neugestaltung der Umgebung umgebaut wurde. Insgesamt fünf Zugänge führen in die mittigen Eingangsbereiche.

Bismarckstraße station was added in 1978 to create an interchange with the new line U7. The aluminium panelling on the walls dates from that period, while the appearance of the retaining wall between the tracks and the colour of the ceiling and pillars has since been modified several times.

Deutsche Oper station was opened in 1906 as a four-track junction, with the main route initially running to Wilhelmplatz (now Richard-Wagner-Platz). This section was last served by shuttle line 5, which closed in 1970 to allow for the construction of line U7. After a fire in July 2000, Deutsche Oper station was restored to its original style, although the usual advertising posters were replaced with Portuguese tile murals. An eastern exit (left) was built in 2006.

Ernst-Reuter-Platz station, the original 1902 terminus then known as Knie, was completely rebuilt in the 1950s as part of a major redevelopment scheme in this part of the city. Five accesses now lead into two entrance areas located in the middle of the station.

14-05-1906 **Deutsche Oper** **U2**

14-12-1902 **Ernst-Reuter-Platz** **U2**

U2 — Zoologischer Garten
11-03-1902

S | U9

Auch wenn hier seit 2006 keine Fernzüge mehr halten, gehört der U-Bhf **Zoologischer Garten** im Herzen der City-West weiterhin zu den meistgenutzten der U2. Die in einfacher Tiefe gelegene Station wurde 1961 im Zuge des Baus der U9, die eine Ebene tiefer kreuzt, umgebaut. So sind hier die für die älteren Stationen typischen preußischen Kappen nur noch über dem Gleisbereich sichtbar. Während sich die Abgänge zur U9 am westlichen Ende befinden, sind die beiden Seitenbahnsteige seit 1928 auch mittig durch einen Tunnel verbunden.

Am **Wittenbergplatz** fährt die U2 auf den beiden ursprünglichen Gleisen der 1902 eröffneten Stammstrecke. 1913 wurde der Bahnhof umgebaut und mit einem Gleis an der Nordseite sowie zwei an der Südseite ergänzt (siehe U1 und U3). Gleichzeitig entstand das wohl imposanteste Zugangsgebäude der Berliner U-Bahn, wie die meisten U-Bahn-Bauten jener Zeit ein Entwurf von Alfred Grenander. Das *Underground*-Schild war 1952 ein Geschenk aus London zum 50. Geburtstag der Berliner U-Bahn, mittlerweile ist sie 111 Jahre alt geworden.

Although no long-distance trains have stopped here since 2006, **Zoologischer Garten**, right in the heart of the 'City West', remains one of the busiest stations on line U2. Located just below street level, the station was rebuilt in 1961 during the construction of line U9, which crosses on the lower level. As a result, the Prussian caps, typical of the older stations, are visible just above the track area. While stairs and escalators down to line U9 are at the western end, the two side platforms have also been connected via a tunnel in the middle of the station since 1928.

At **Wittenbergplatz**, line U2 runs on the two original tracks laid in 1902. In 1913, the station was enlarged with another track on the north side and two on the south side (see U1 and U3). At the same time, Alfred Grenander, then responsible for most U-Bahn structures, designed what is probably the U-Bahn's most impressive station building. The Underground roundel was a gift from London for the 50th anniversary of the Berlin U-Bahn in 1952; in the meantime it has become 111 years old.

Zoologischer Garten

11-03-1902 | **Wittenbergplatz** | U2

U1 U3

U2 — Nollendorfplatz

11-03-1902

▶ U1 U3 U4

Den Hochbahnhof **Nollendorfplatz** zierte bis zum Zweiten Weltkrieg eine prächtige Kuppel. Zum 100. Geburtstag der Strecke wurde sie 2002 in stilisierter Form wiedererrichtet. Gleichzeitig wurden seitlich Aufzüge angebaut. Von 1972 bis 1993, als der Abschnitt stillgelegt war, fungierte dieser Bahnhof als Flohmarkt. Er war mit dem benachbarten Türkischen Basar im Hochbahnhof Bülowstraße durch eine Nostalgiestraßenbahn auf U-Bahn-Gleisen verbunden.

Bülowstraße gehört zu den besterhaltenen Hochbahnhöfen der Strecke von 1902, auch wenn im Zweiten Weltkrieg einige Jugendstilelemente verloren gingen. Dasselbe gilt für die reichlich verzierten Stützen des anschließenden Viadukts. Beides stammt von Bruno Möhring. Die Hochlage erlaubte auch hier 1994 den einfachen Einbau von Aufzügen.

Der Turmbahnhof **Gleisdreieck** wurde 1912 nach einem schweren Unfall an der Stelle eines tatsächlichen Gleisdreiecks errichtet. In den späten 1980er Jahren wurde der ungenutzte untere Bahnsteig für Tests der sog. „M-Bahn" (Magnetbahn) verwendet.

Nollendorfplatz

Before World War II, the elevated **Nollendorfplatz** station boasted an impressive cupola, which was rebuilt in a stylised form for the line's 100th birthday in 2002. At the same time, lifts were added to the sides of the station. From 1972 to 1993, when this elevated section was shut down, the station housed a flea market. It was connected to the neighbouring Turkish bazaar at Bülowstraße by a museum tram on metro tracks.

Bülowstraße is one of the best preserved elevated stations of the 1902 line, although during World War II some Art Nouveau elements were lost. The same applies to the richly ornamented pillars of the connecting viaduct. The station and viaduct were designed by Bruno Möhring. Adding lifts on the sides of this elevated station was an easy task in 1994.

The bi-level **Gleisdreieck** station was built in 1912 after a serious accident at the site of the original triangular junction. In the late 1980s, the then unused lower platform was used to test the so-called 'M-Bahn' (a maglev railway).

Bülowstraße

Bülowstraße — U2
11-03-1902

Gleisdreieck — U2
03-11-1912

U2 — Mendelssohn-Bartholdy-Park
01-10-1998

Der U-Bhf **Mendelssohn-Bartholdy-Park** wurde 1998 unter laufendem Betrieb im südlichen Bereich des Potsdamer-Platz-Areals in die bestehende Strecke eingebaut. 2008/09 wurde die zuvor offene Tunnelrampe mit einem Hotel überbaut.

Am **Potsdamer Platz** lag Berlins erster unterirdischer Bahnhof. Der ursprüngliche wurde allerdings 1907 im Zuge des Weiterbaus Richtung Innenstadt durch den heutigen, ca. 200 m weiter nordöstlich gelegenen ersetzt. Die Grenze zwischen Ost und West verlief genau über den Potsdamer Platz, weshalb der U-Bahnhof zu Mauerzeiten für keine der beiden Seiten nutzbar war, er diente jedoch der BVG-Ost als Abstellanlage. Die Station wurde zur Wiedereröffnung 1993 saniert, der Aufzug (rechts) 2009 nachgerüstet.

Die einzige Ost-Berliner Kleinprofillinie endete am heutigen U-Bhf **Mohrenstraße**, der jedoch im Laufe der Geschichte die verschiedensten Namen trug (siehe Anhang). Dass beim Wiederaufbau nach dem Zweiten Weltkrieg roter Marmor aus der benachbarten Reichskanzlei verwendet wurde, kann nicht belegt werden.

Mendelssohn-Bartholdy-Park station was added in the southern part of the Potsdamer Platz area in 1998 without disrupting service on the recently restored line. In 2008/09, a hotel was built above what had been an open tunnel ramp.

Potsdamer Platz was Berlin's first underground station, although today's station is located some 200 m further northeast of the original station, which was replaced in 1907 when the line was extended towards the city centre. Because the borderline between East and West ran right across Potsdamer Platz, the underground station could not be used by either side, but it served the eastern BVG for stabling trains. The station was refurbished for its reopening in 1993, and a lift was retrofitted in 2009 (above).

East Berlin's only small-profile line terminated at today's *Mohrenstraße* station, which has had many different names in its history (see Annex). It cannot be verified if red marble from the nearby Chancellery was used in the station's reconstruction after World War II.

| 18-02-1902 | **Potsdamer Platz** | U2 |

▶ Ⓢ

| 01-10-1908 | **Mohrenstraße** | U2 |

U2 — Stadtmitte — 01-10-1908

▶ U6

Sehr bescheiden präsentiert sich der U-Bhf **Stadtmitte** zwischen Friedrichstraße und Gendarmenmarkt. Wie bei der U6, die man über den „Mäusetunnel" erreicht, findet man hier an beiden Bahnsteigenden jeweils zwei hintereinander liegende Treppen in Straßenmitte.

Der nur 385 m weiter östlich gelegene U-Bhf **Hausvogteiplatz** weist einen merklich gekrümmten Bahnsteig auf. Wie Stadtmitte ähnelte er ursprünglich dem historisch wiederhergestellten Bahnhof Spittelmarkt. Heute zieren historische Fotografien der Umgebung die Seitenwände und der östliche Ausgang zum namensgebenden Platz erinnert mit Inschriften an die aus diesem Viertel deportierten Juden.

Der U-Bhf **Spittelmarkt** bekam 2005/06 sein ursprüngliches Aussehen zurück. Während die Wände dem Standardtyp für diesen Abschnitt (hier mit der Kennfarbe Blau) entsprachen, unterschied sich dieser Bahnhof durch die zahlreichen Tageslichtöffnungen zum Kupfergraben hin, die im Krieg zugemauert und nun anlässlich der Renovierung wieder geöffnet wurden. Die Wände schmücken nun historische Ansichten der Umgebung.

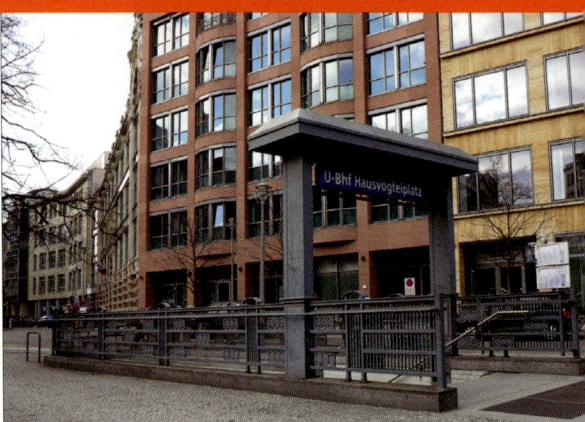

The rather simple **Stadtmitte** station is located between Friedrichstraße and Gendarmenmarkt. Like on line U6, which is connected via the so-called 'mouse tunnel', two staggered sets of stairs leading to the middle of the street can be found at either end of the platform.

Hausvogteiplatz station lies only 385 m further east and features a noticeably curved platform. Like Stadtmitte, it used to be similar to the recently restored station at Spittelmarkt. Today, old photographs of the area adorn the walls, while at the eastern exit (above) leading to the eponymous square, inscriptions commemorate the Jews deported from the neighbourhood.

Spittelmarkt station was restored to its original appearance in 2005/06. While the walls correspond to the standard type established for this section (here with blue frames), the station differed from the rest in having numerous side openings towards the Kupfergraben, which had been bricked up in the War and were now reopened. Images on the walls now depict historical views of the area.

01-10-1908 **Hausvogteiplatz** **U2**

01-10-1908 **Spittelmarkt** **U2**

U2 — Märkisches Museum
01-07-1913

Der U-Bhf **Märkisches Museum** erinnert eher an die Pariser Métro als an die Berliner U-Bahn. Wegen der nördlich anschließenden Unterfahrung der Spree entstand eine sehr hohe stützenlose Bahnsteighalle mit einem verfliesten Gewölbe. Zum 750. Geburtstag Berlins 1987 wurden stilisierte Stadtpläne an den Wänden angebracht.

Ähnlich wie Sophie-Charlotte-Platz im Westen wurde der U-Bhf **Klosterstraße** 1987 mit Motiven des städtischen Schienenverkehrs gestaltet. Auch die gelbliche Beleuchtung versetzt den Fahrgast in eine frühere Zeit. Sehenswert sind außerdem die Zwischengeschosse mit Motiven aus dem Thronsaal von Babylon, dessen Original im Pergamon-Museum zu bewundern ist. Diese Station war als Verzweigungsbahnhof mit drei Gleisen konzipiert, woraus sich der heute sehr breite Bahnsteig mit den nicht mittig angeordneten Stützen erklärt.

Am **Alexanderplatz** kann man sowohl zu zwei anderen U-Bahn-Linien als auch zur S-Bahn und Regionalbahn umsteigen. Der U2-Bahnsteig wurde häufig für künstlerische Aktivitäten zur Verfügung gestellt. Die Neuverfliesung von 2006 lehnt sich an das Original an.

Klosterstraße

Märkisches Museum station is more reminiscent of the Paris Métro than the Berlin U-Bahn. Because the line crosses under the Spree River just north of the station, a rather high column-free platform hall with a tiled vaulted ceiling was created. For the city's 750th birthday in 1987, stylised maps were mounted on the walls.

Rather like Sophie-Charlotte-Platz station in the West, **Klosterstraße** station was enhanced with urban rail transport motifs in 1987. The yellowish lighting transports passengers back into the past. The two mezzanines feature themes from the throne room of Babylon, the original of which can be seen in the Pergamon Museum. The station was designed as a junction with three tracks, which explains the rather wide platform and why the supports are not positioned centrally.

At **Alexanderplatz**, passengers can transfer to two other U-Bahn lines as well as the S-Bahn and regional trains. The U2 platform used to be regularly available for artistic works. The 2006 retiling kept to the original style of the station.

01-07-1913 | **Klosterstraße** | U2

01-07-1913 | **Alexanderplatz** | U2

U2 — Rosa-Luxemburg-Platz — 01-07-1913

Der U-Bhf **Rosa-Luxemburg-Platz** wurde zum 750-Jahr-Jubiläum der Stadt Berlin 1987 mit Collagen, die Persönlichkeiten der deutschen Geschichte zeigten, verziert, darunter Albert Einstein, Käthe Kollwitz und Karl Liebknecht. Diese Wandbilder wurden jedoch wegen wiederholtem Vandalismus vor einigen Jahren entfernt.

Ursprünglich muss der U-Bhf **Senefelderplatz** dem U-Bhf Spittelmarkt geähnelt haben, doch in den 1970er Jahren wurde auch hier eine neue Wandverfliesung angebracht, deren Grundfarbe sich jedoch an das Farbkonzept Grenanders anlehnt. An den Wandfliesen kann man auch erkennen, dass die Decke Richtung Norden leicht ansteigt. Anders als die Hochbahnhöfe der Stammstrecke von 1902 wurden die beiden oberirdischen Stationen in der Schönhauser Allee wie auch die unterirdischen jener Zeit mit einem Mittelbahnsteig errichtet. Im gut erhaltenen Bahnhof **Eberswalder Straße** wurde 2010 die Beleuchtung verbessert und ein Aufzug eingebaut.

Eberswalder Straße

For the city's 750th anniversary in 1987, **Rosa-Luxemburg-Platz** station was enhanced with collage works depicting personalities from German history, including Albert Einstein, Käthe Kollwitz and Karl Liebknecht. These murals were removed a few years ago because of repeated vandalism.

The original **Senefelderplatz** station must have been similar to Spittelmarkt station, but in the 1970s the walls were retiled, though following the colour scheme developed by Grenander. The wall tiling reveals that the ceiling rises slowly towards the northern end of the station.

Unlike the elevated stations on the original line from 1902, the two above-ground stations along Schönhauser Allee, just like the underground stations of the time, were built with island platforms. At the well-preserved **Eberswalder Straße** station, the lighting was improved and a lift was installed in 2010.

01-07-1913 **Senefelderplatz** U2

01-07-1913 **Eberswalder Straße** U2

U2 — Schönhauser Allee — 01-07-1913

Der Hochbahnhof **Schönhauser Allee** ähnelt seinem südlichen Nachbarn und war 17 Jahre nördliche Endstation der Linie A. 1962, kurz nach der Trennung des S-Bahn-Netzes durch den Bau der Berliner Mauer, wurde ein direkter Übergang zur S-Bahn eingerichtet, die hier im Einschnitt verläuft.

Jahrzehntelang endete die Linie A, später die U2, am U-Bhf **Vinetastraße** in Pankow. Die Station wurde 1985 umgestaltet und 2010 saniert, wobei nun die preußischen Kappen wieder freigelegt wurden. Über das mittig angeordnete Zwischengeschoss erreicht man Ausgänge in Straßenseitenlage sowie direkte Aufgänge zur Straßenbahnhaltestelle.

Im Jahr 2000 erreichte die U2 schließlich den S-Bahnhof **Pankow**. Die kurze Verlängerung war bereits zu DDR-Zeiten begonnen worden, denn nördlich von Vinetastraße sollte eine neue Betriebswerkstatt entstehen. Die Gestaltung des Endbahnhofs ist im typischen Stil der späten 1990er Jahre gehalten. Eine Verlängerung bis Pankow Kirche wurde abermals verschoben.

Vinetastraße

The elevated **Schönhauser Allee** station is similar to its southern neighbour. For 17 years, it used to be the northern terminus of line A. In 1962, shortly after the S-Bahn network was split following the erection of the Berlin Wall, a direct transfer tunnel was built between the U-Bahn and the S-Bahn, which runs in a trench at this point.

For many decades, line A, and later line U2, used to terminate at **Vinetastraße** in Pankow. The station was rebuilt in 1985 and renovated in 2010, when the typical Prussian caps were uncovered. Exits lead from the centrally located mezzanine to the pavements, but also directly to the tram stop.

In 2000, line U2 finally reached the S-Bahn station **Pankow**. This short extension had been started during GDR times to serve a new maintenance facility then planned north of Vinetastraße station. The design of the present terminus is typical of the late 1990s. An extension to Pankow Kirche has once again been shelved.

29-06-1930 **Vinetastraße** **U2**

16-09-2000 **Pankow** **U2**

U3 — Krumme Lanke – Nollendorfplatz

Oskar-Helene-Heim > Thielplatz

Die heutige U3 entspricht weitgehend der „Wilmersdorf-Dahlemer Schnellbahn", die 1913 als Abzweig der Stammstrecke von 1902 durch die damals noch unabhängige Stadt Wilmersdorf unterirdisch und durch die benachbarte Domäne Dahlem im offenen Einschnitt gebaut wurde, was ihr selbst im Kleinprofilnetz einen eigenen Charakter verleiht. Diese Strecke wurde 1929 bis zu ihrem heutigen Endpunkt Krumme Lanke verlängert.

Während man die unterirdischen Stationen im wohlhabenden Wilmersdorf abwechslungsreich und prunkvoll gestalten ließ, sind auf dem Dahlemer Abschnitt die unterschiedlichen, jedoch meist im Landhausstil gehaltenen Eingangsgebäude hervorzuheben. Die Siedlungsstruktur ist in dieser Gegend bis heute eher aufgelockert, doch sorgen die zahlreichen Studenten der hier ansässigen Freien Universität für eine Auslastung der Züge während der Vorlesungszeiten.

Today's line U3 largely corresponds to the 'Wilmersdorf-Dahlemer Schnellbahn', which was opened in 1913 as a branch of the original metro line from 1902. It was built underground through the then independent town of Wilmersdorf, and in an open trench through neighbouring Dahlem, in Berlin a rather unusual type of alignment even for the small-profile network. The line was extended to its current terminus Krumme Lanke in 1929.

While the underground stations in affluent Wilmersdorf boast varied and opulent designs, the Dahlem section is distinguished by its country-style entrance buildings. The urban structure in this area is still rather sparse, but the Freie Universität's numerous students keep trains busy during semester time.

Fehrbelliner Platz

U3

12.2 km (5 km oberirdisch | *surface*)
(0.8 km gemeinsam mit U1 | *shared with line U1*)
15 Bahnhöfe | *stations*

12-10-1913: Wittenbergplatz – Thielplatz
24-10-1926: Wittenbergplatz – Nollendorfplatz [– Gleisdreieck]
22-12-1929: Thielplatz – Krumme Lanke
01-06-1959: [X] Nürnberger Platz
02-06-1959: + Spichernstraße
08-05-1961: + Augsburger Straße

[X] Schließung | *Closure*

Der Ast nach Krumme Lanke wurde bis in die 1950er Jahre meist als Linie AII bezeichnet, wobei die Linienführung östlich des Wittenbergplatzes von Zeit zu Zeit geändert wurde. Ab 1966 fuhren die Züge von Krumme Lanke als Linie 2 bis 1972 über Bülowstraße zum Gleisdreieck, dann nur noch bis Wittenbergplatz, ab 1993 als U1 zum Schlesischen Tor bzw. ab 1995 zur Warschauer Straße und schließlich seit 2004 als U3 zum Nollendorfplatz, wobei zwischen Wittenbergplatz und der Endstation die Gleise der U1 benutzt werden. Am Nollendorfplatz kommen die Züge der U3 zwar auf dem Gleis der U1 an, fahren dann aber vom lange ungenutzten zweiten Gleis auf der unteren Ebene ab, das für die U4 vorgesehen war.

Mittelfristig könnte die U3 um eine Station von Krumme Lanke bis zum S-Bahnhof Mexikoplatz verlängert werden (850 m).

Until the 1950s, the branch to Krumme Lanke was known as line AII, with the route east of Wittenbergplatz changing from time to time. Trains from Krumme Lanke operated as line 2 to Gleisdreieck via Bülowstraße from 1966 until 1972, when they were cut back to Wittenbergplatz; as line U1 to Schlesisches Tor from 1993 and to Warschauer Straße from 1995; before finally being labelled U3 in 2004. Inbound trains now terminate at Nollendorfplatz, sharing tracks with line U1 between Wittenbergplatz and the terminus. At Nollendorfplatz, U3 trains arrive on the U1 track but depart from the long-unused second track on the lower level, which was intended for line U4.

In the mid-term future, line U3 could be extended by one station from Krumme Lanke to the S-Bahn station Mexikoplatz (850 m).

Dahlem-Dorf

U3 — Krumme Lanke — 22-12-1929

Das hufeisenförmige Empfangsgebäude an der Endstation **Krumme Lanke** (benannt nach einem nahegelegenen See) wurde 1989 nach dem von Alfred Grenander im Stil der Neuen Sachlichkeit errichteten Original neu aufgebaut.

Der eigenartige Name der Station **Onkel Toms Hütte** leitet sich von einem Gasthaus her, das ein Amerikaner namens Tom in der Nähe hatte und dem die Leute aus dieser Gegend den Namen des berühmten Romans von Harriet Beecher Stowe gaben. Zwei Jahre nach Eröffnung des Bahnhofs kamen die für die Berliner U-Bahn einzigartigen Ladenpassagen hinzu, die parallel zu den Gleisen verlaufen. Der Bahnsteigbereich ist mit Glas überdacht.

Nur der Schriftzug an der Hausfront verrät, dass es sich hier um den Zugang zum U-Bhf **Oskar-Helene-Heim** (benannt nach einem ehem. Krankenhaus) und nicht um ein Landhaus handelt. Der Innenraum hingegen entspricht dem Gestaltungsstil der U-Bahn aus den 1920er Jahren (unten).

Krumme Lanke

The horseshoe-shaped entrance building at **Krumme Lanke** (named after a nearby lake) was rebuilt in 1989 following the original designed by Alfred Grenander in New Functionalism style.

The curious name of next station, **Onkel Toms Hütte**, comes from a nearby inn once owned by an American named Tom, whose establishment the local people referred to as Uncle Tom's Cabin after the famous novel by Harriet Beecher Stowe. Two years after the opening of the station, a peculiar shopping mall was added parallel to the tracks; the platform area was covered with a glass roof.

The lettering on the façade is the only indication that this is the entrance to **Oskar-Helene-Heim** station (named after a former hospital), and not a country house. Inside, however, a ticket hall in typical 1920s U-Bahn style can be found (left).

Oskar-Helene-Heim

22-12-1929 **Onkel Toms Hütte** `U3`

22-12-1929 **Oskar-Helene-Heim** `U3`

U3   Thielplatz   12-10-1913

Das östliche Eingangsgebäude am U-Bhf **Thielplatz** mit seiner riesigen Uhr über dem Portal wurde einem Landhaus im nahen Nikolassee nachgebaut. Der westliche Ausgang kam erst 1980 hinzu und lehnt sich architektonisch an den östlichen an. 16 Jahre lang war Thielplatz Endstation der „Wilmersdorf-Dahlemer Schnellbahn".

Am U-Bhf **Dahlem-Dorf** erinnert selbst der Stationsname an die ländliche Vergangenheit. Das Eingangsgebäude wurde im norddeutschen Landhausstil als Holzfachwerkbau mit Reetdach errichtet. Auch der Innenraum mit seiner bemalten Decke (rechts) gleicht eher einem Jagdschloss als einem U-Bahnhof. Nach einem Brand im Jahr 1980 wurde das Gebäude originalgetreu wiederaufgebaut. Der Aufzug am westlichen Bahnsteigende kam 2004 hinzu (unten).

Ohne das U an der Fassade könnte man meinen, der Eingang des U-Bhf **Podbielskiallee** führe zu einer mittelalterlichen Burg. Diese Station liegt direkt am Tunnelmund der U3, ab hier geht es unterirdisch weiter durch Wilmersdorf.

The eastern entrance building at **Thielplatz** station with its huge clock above the portal is a copy of a mansion in nearby Nikolassee; the western exit was added in a similar style in 1980. For the first 16 years, Thielplatz was the end-of-line for the 'Wilmersdorf-Dahlemer Schnellbahn'.

At **Dahlem-Dorf** [Dahlem Village], even the station name reminds us of the area's rural past, with the entrance building in North German cottage style with a thatched roof. The interior with its painted wooden ceiling (above) looks more like a hunting lodge than a metro station. After a fire in 1980, the entrance building was rebuilt in its original style. The lift at the western end of the platform was added in 2004 (left).

If it were not for the U on the façade, the big gate at **Podbielskiallee** could almost be the entrance to a medieval castle. The station is located right at the U3 tunnel portal, with the rest of the line through Wilmersdorf being underground.

12-10-1913 **Dahlem-Dorf** **U3**

12-10-1913 **Podbielskiallee** **U3**

43

U3 — Breitenbachplatz — 12-10-1913

Wie alle U-Bahnhöfe in der einst selbständigen Stadt Wilmersdorf wurde auch der U-Bhf **Breitenbachplatz** von Wilhelm Leitgebel gestaltet. Hervorzuheben sind die massiven Steinsäulen und Verzierungen, u.a. mit Tiermotiven, an den Wänden. Die Bilder mit Eisenbahnmotiven von J. Szymczak in den Wandnischen kamen erst 1988 hinzu – Paul von Breitenbach war Präsident der preußischen Eisenbahn.

Auch im U-Bhf **Rüdesheimer Platz** kontrastieren die schweren Steinsäulen mit kleinteiligen Jugendstilverzierungen an Decke und Seitenwänden, hier mit Motiven aus dem Weinbau (rechts), schließlich liegt der U-Bahnhof im Rheingauviertel, das nach einem bekannten Weinbaugebiet in Hessen benannt ist.

Höhepunkt der „Wilmersdorf-Dahlemer Schnellbahn" ist sicherlich der U-Bhf **Heidelberger Platz**, der aufgrund seiner größeren Tiefenlage, bedingt durch die Unterfahrung der im Einschnitt verlaufenden Ringbahn, ein prächtiges Deckengewölbe aufweist. An den Wänden hängen Fotografien der Stadt Heidelberg.

Rüdesheimer Platz

Like all the underground stations in the once independent town of Wilmersdorf, **Breitenbachplatz** station was designed by Wilhelm Leitgebel and features massive stone columns and rich ornamentation (e.g. animal motifs) on the walls. The paintings, added by J. Szymczak in 1988, have railway themes as Paul von Breitenbach was president of the Prussian Railways.

At **Rüdesheimer Platz**, the heavy stone columns contrast with art-nouveau elements on the ceiling and walls, here with grapes (above) — the station is located in the Rheingauviertel, a neighbourhood named after a well-known wine-growing region in the State of Hesse.

The absolute highlight of the 'Wilmersdorf-Dahlemer Schnellbahn' is certainly **Heidelberger Platz** station; it is located at greater depth than usual due to the fact that the line passes under the orbital S-Bahn line, and the station therefore features impressive high vaults. The walls are decorated with large photographs of Heidelberg.

12-10-1913 **Rüdesheimer Platz** **U3**

12-10-1913 **Heidelberger Platz** **U3**

45

Fehrbelliner Platz

U3 — 12-10-1913

▶ U7

Bis 1929 musste man am **Fehrbelliner Platz** umsteigen, wenn man Richtung Thielplatz weiterfahren wollte, da auf dem äußeren Abschnitt kein Bedarf an langen Zügen bestand. Seit 1971 kann man zur U7 auf der unteren Ebene umsteigen. Zu jener Zeit entstand auch das markante rote Eingangsgebäude (auch S. 97). An den Wänden hängen seit 1978 Fotografien von Heinrich Zille.

Im U-Bhf **Hohenzollernplatz** dominieren wieder die massiven Steinsäulen. Die Seitenwände zieren Ansichten der Hohenzollern-Stammburg im heutigen Baden-Württemberg. Die Hohenzollern waren die letzte in Deutschland regierende Dynastie.

Im Zuge des Baus der U9 wurde 1959 die Station Nürnberger Platz geschlossen und etwa 200 m weiter südwestlich durch die neue Umsteigestation **Spichernstraße** ersetzt. Da sich die Seitenbahnsteige in einfacher Tiefenlage befinden, muss man vom stadteinwärtigen Bahnsteig erst die Gleise unterqueren, um zur Verteilerebene und schließlich zur U9 zu kommen. Stadtauswärts ist das Umsteigen wesentlich bequemer.

Until 1929, all passengers heading for Thielplatz had to change trains at **Fehrbelliner Platz** as there was insufficient demand for long trains on the outer section. Since 1971, transfer to line U7 has been provided on the lower level. The iconic red entrance building (see also p. 97) was opened at the same time. In 1978, photographs by Heinrich Zille were mounted on the walls.

Hohenzollernplatz station is again dominated by massive stone pillars, while the side walls depict views of Hohenzollern Castle in Baden-Württemberg, Southern Germany. The Hohenzollern dynasty was the last to reign in Germany.

In conjunction with the construction of line U9, Nürnberger Platz station was closed in 1959 and replaced by a new interchange station at **Spichernstraße**, some 200 m further southwest. As the side platforms are just below street level, inbound passengers have to pass under the tracks to reach the distribution level and eventually line U9; transfers in the outbound direction are more convenient.

| 12-10-1913 | **Hohenzollernplatz** | **U3** |

| 02-06-1959 | **Spichernstraße** | **U3** |

47

U3 — Augsburger Straße — 08-05-1961

Der U-Bhf **Augsburger Straße** wurde 1961 zwischen Spichernstraße und Wittenbergplatz eingefügt, nachdem der U-Bhf Nürnberger Platz 1959 geschlossen worden war. Die Seitenbahnsteige sind hier mittig durch einen Fußgängertunnel verbunden.

Am U-Bhf **Wittenbergplatz** kann man von der U3 in beiden Richtungen am selben Bahnsteig gegenüber bequem in die U2 umsteigen. Stadtauswärts teilen sich die U1 und die U3 dasselbe Gleis. Diese Station entstand bereits 1902 auf Berlins ältester U-Bahn-Strecke als einfache Zwischenstation mit Seitenbahnsteigen, jedoch wurde sie 1913 auf fünf Gleise erweitert, um die beiden neuen westlichen Äste zum Kurfürstendamm sowie nach Wilmersdorf aufnehmen zu können.

Der doppelstöckige unterirdische Teil des U-Bhf **Nollendorfplatz** entstand 1926 im Zuge des Baus der Entlastungsstrecke zum Gleisdreieck. Auf der oberen Ebene kann man auf demselben Bahnsteig gegenüber in die hier wendende U4 umsteigen. Mitte der 1990er Jahre wurden die Wände nach dem originalen Vorbild neu verfliest. Der östliche Ausgang samt Aufzug steht seit 1998 zur Verfügung.

Nollendorfplatz

Augsburger Straße station was added between Wittenbergplatz and Spichernstraße in 1961 after the closing of Nürnberger Platz station in 1959. The side platforms are linked via a pedestrian tunnel in the middle of the station.

At **Wittenbergplatz**, cross-platform interchange is available between lines U2 and U3 in both directions. Outbound U1 and U3 trains share the same track. Opened in 1902 as part of Berlin's original metro line, the station initially functioned as a simple through station with side platforms, but in 1913 it was enlarged to accommodate two additional western branches, one along Kurfürstendamm and another to Wilmersdorf; it now has five tracks.

The bi-level underground portion of **Nollendorfplatz** station was built together with the relief route to Gleisdreieck in 1926. On the upper level, cross-platform interchange to line U4, which reverses here, is possible. The walls were retiled in the mid-1990s in the original style of the station. The eastern exit and a lift were added in 1998.

Wittenbergplatz

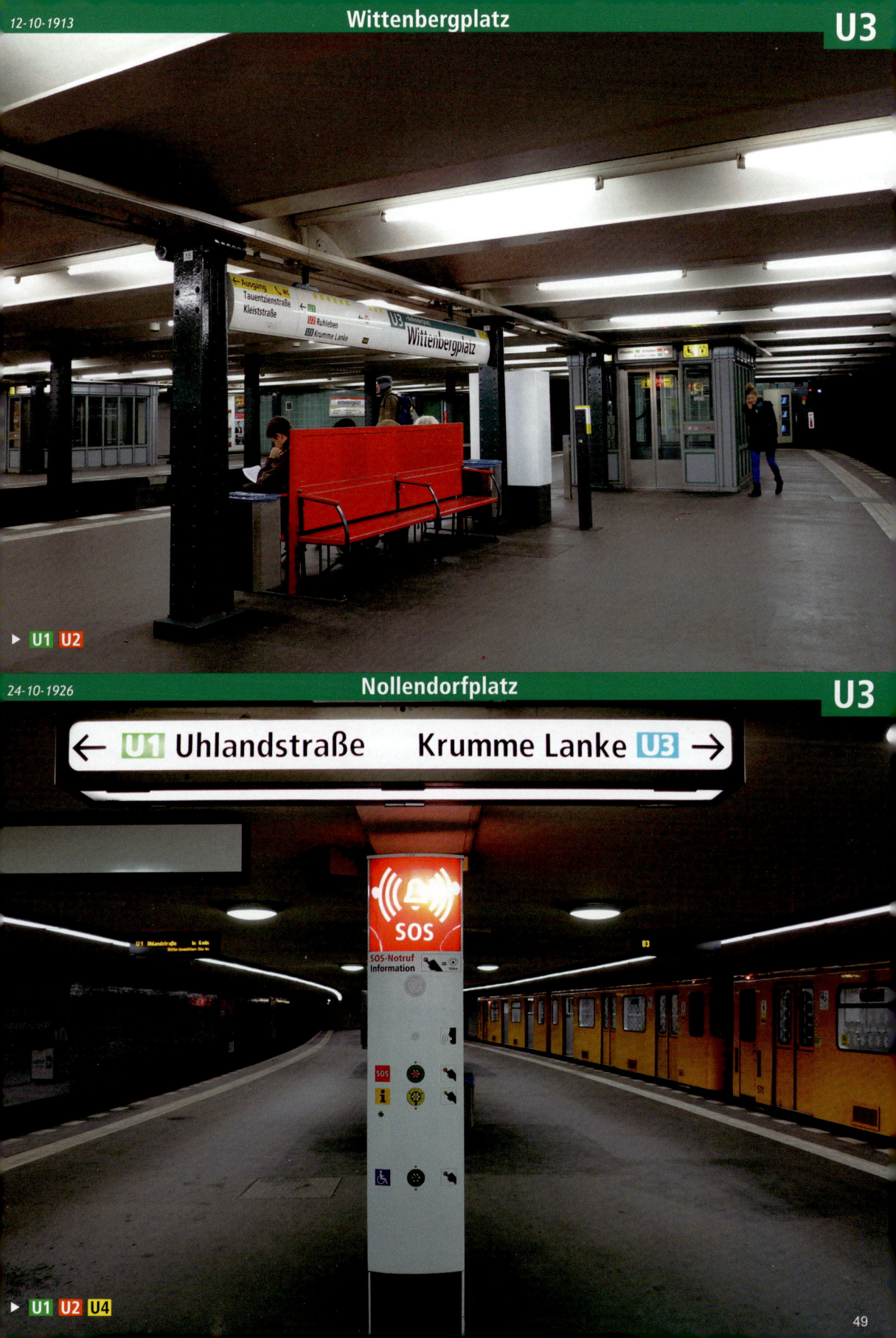

12-10-1913 — **U3**

▶ U1 U2

Nollendorfplatz

24-10-1926 — **U3**

▶ U1 U2 U4

U4 Nollendorfplatz – Innsbrucker Platz

Rathaus Schöneberg

Die „Schöneberger U-Bahn" wurde zwar von der damals eigenständigen Stadt Schöneberg errichtet, doch folgte sie den Parametern der Siemens'schen „Hoch- und Untergrundbahn" und wurde auch von dieser betrieben. Deshalb war es nach der Gründung Groß-Berlins auch nicht schwierig, sie 1926 am Nollendorfplatz (ursprünglich lag die Endstation südlich des Hochbahnhofs) an das bestehende Berliner Kleinprofilnetz anzuschließen und als Teil der Linie B (heutige U1 zur Warschauer Straße) zu betreiben. Seit 1965 pendelt sie nun als Linie 4 bzw. U4 wieder zwischen Nollendorfplatz und Innsbrucker Platz, meist nur mit 2-Wagen-Zügen.

The 'Schöneberger U-Bahn' was built by what was then the independent city of Schöneberg, but following the parameters of Siemens' 'Hoch- und Untergrundbahn'; it was also operated by this company. With the founding of Greater Berlin, it therefore became possible in 1926 to connect it to Berlin's existing small-profile network at Nollendorfplatz (the original terminus was located south of the elevated station), and operate it as part of line B (today's U1 to Warschauer Straße). Since 1965, it has again been shuttling as line 4 or U4 between Nollendorfplatz and Innsbrucker Platz, usually only with 2-car trains.

Die U4 teilt sich den doppelstöckigen unterirdischen Bahnhof am **Nollendorfplatz** mit der U1 und U3. Sie benutzt dabei nur die südliche Bahnsteigkante der oberen Ebene der 1999 renovierten Anlage.

Am **Viktoria-Luise-Platz** kam neben dem klassischen Eingangsportal am namensgebenden Platz (siehe Seite 3) 2005 ein zweiter Ausgang in der Motzstraße hinzu (links).

At **Nollendorfplatz**, line U4 shares the bi-level underground portion of the station with lines U1 and U3. It only makes use of the southern platform edge on the upper level. The station was refurbished in 1999.

Viktoria-Luise-Platz station, which features a classic entrance portal at the square of that name (see page 3), was complemented in 2005 with a second entrance located on Motzstraße (left).

U4
2.9 km (gänzlich unterirdisch | *completely underground*)
5 Bahnhöfe | *stations*
01-12-1910: Nollendorfplatz – Innsbrucker Platz

01-12-1910 **Nollendorfplatz** U4

U1 U2 U3

01-12-1910 **Viktoria-Luise-Platz** U4

51

U4 Bayerischer Platz 01-12-1910

▶ U7

Wie die benachbarten Stationen ist auch der U-Bhf **Bayerischer Platz** weitgehend original erhalten, nur der südliche Zugangsbereich wurde 1971 im Zuge des Baus der U7 umgestaltet. Aus den 1980er Jahren stammen die Aluminiumschilder zwischen den Mittelstützen. Vielleicht wählte man hier bereits Anfang des 20. Jahrhunderts bewusst das allgemein mit Bayern assoziierte Blau als Kennfarbe für den U-Bahnhof.

Eine Besonderheit im Berliner U-Bahn-Netz stellt der U-Bhf **Rathaus Schöneberg** dar, da er quer zu einer Geländemulde liegt und deshalb vom Bahnsteig aus durch große Fenster einen Blick in den Schöneberger Stadtpark ermöglicht (s. S. 50). Statt eines zweiten Ausgangs wurde ein Notausgang direkt in den Park errichtet.

Am südlichen Endpunkt **Innsbrucker Platz**, der wie seine drei nördlichen Nachbarn in einfacher Tiefenlage liegt, kam 2003 am nördlichen Bahnsteigende ein zweiter Ausgang hinzu (rechts). Vom südlichen Verteiler führt seit 2005 ein Aufzug an die Oberfläche direkt vor den Eingang zur S-Bahn.

Like the neighbouring stations, **Bayerischer Platz** station is largely preserved in its original style, with only the southern entrance area having been remodelled in 1971 in conjunction with the construction of line U7. The aluminium station signs between the central supports date from the 1980s. It is possible that already in the early 20th Century, blue was deliberately chosen for this station as this colour is generally associated with Bavaria.

Rathaus Schöneberg is certainly unique among Berlin's U-Bahn stations in that it cuts through a depression, thus providing a view of Schöneberg's city park from the platform through the large windows (see p. 50). Instead of a second regular exit, an emergency exit leads directly into the park.

At the southern terminus **Innsbrucker Platz**, which like its three northern neighbours lies just below street level, a second exit was added at the northern end of the platform (above) in 2003. In 2005, a lift from the southern vestibule to the surface directly in front of the entrance to the S-Bahn was installed.

| 01-12-1910 | Rathaus Schöneberg | U4 |

| 01-12-1910 | Innsbrucker Platz | U4 |

U5   Hauptbahnhof – Hönow

Elsterwerdaer Platz > Wuhletal

Der erste Abschnitt der heutigen Linie U5 wurde 1930 als Linie E vom Alexanderplatz nach Friedrichsfelde in Betrieb genommen. Diese 7,8 km lange Strecke wurde in vier Jahren gebaut und verläuft größtenteils unter der Karl-Marx-Allee und der Frankfurter Allee vom Stadtzentrum Richtung Osten.

    Mit dem Bau der Berliner Mauer im August 1961 wurde die Linie E zur einzigen Großprofillinie auf Ost-Berliner Gebiet (die beiden anderen wurden zu Transitlinien West-Berlins) und als solche wurde sie im Jahr 1973 um eine Station bis Tierpark verlängert. Erst in den letzten Jahren der DDR kam eine längere Neubaustrecke hinzu, deren Ziel es war, die entstehenden Wohngebiete am östlichen Stadtrand in Hellersdorf anzuschließen. Diese Verlängerung sollte ursprünglich ein weiterer S-Bahn-Ast werden, doch dann entschied man sich für eine Erweiterung der

The first section of today's line U5 opened in 1930 as line E, which connected Alexanderplatz to Friedrichsfelde. Built in four years, this 7.8 km line runs from the city centre towards the east, mostly under Karl-Marx-Allee and Frankfurter Allee.

    The erection of the Berlin Wall in August 1961 left line E the only large-profile line in East Berlin territory (the other two became non-stopping West Berlin lines), which was then extended in 1973 by adding a new station at Tierpark. It was only in the last years of the GDR that a longer extension was built to connect the emerging housing estates in Hellersdorf on the eastern outskirts of the city. Originally planned as another S-Bahn branch, an U-Bahn extension with a rather S-Bahn-like alignment was built instead.

U5   U55

18.4 km (9.4 km oberirdisch | *surface*)
+ U55: 1.5 km
+ 2.2 km im Bau | *under construction*
23 Bahnhöfe | *stations* (+ 3 im Bau | *under construction*)

21-12-1930: Alexanderplatz – Friedrichsfelde
25-06-1973: Friedrichsfelde – Tierpark
01-07-1988: Tierpark – Elsterwerdaer Platz
01-07-1989: Elsterwerdaer Platz – Hönow
08-08-2009: Hauptbahnhof – Brandenburger Tor (U55)

~2019: Brandenburger Tor – Alexanderplatz

Lichtenberg

U-Bahn-Linie, die allerdings eine sehr S-Bahn-artige Trassierung aufweist.

Schon bei ihrer Inbetriebnahme 1930 war eine Verlängerung dieser Radiallinie Richtung Westen geplant, jedoch wurde diese erst nach dem Fall der Mauer im Zusammenhang mit dem Bau des Regierungsviertels und des neuen Hauptbahnhofs in Angriff genommen. Aus finanziellen Gründen wurden die Bauarbeiten allerdings zwischenzeitlich eingestellt, so dass erst 2009 der westliche Abschnitt als U55 in Betrieb gehen konnte. Der Lückenschluss zwischen Brandenburger Tor und Alexanderplatz, dessen Bau 2012 wieder voll aufgenommen wurde, soll nach heutigem Stand im Jahr 2019 geschafft sein. Einst war geplant, die U5 über Turmstraße (U9) und Jungfernheide (U7) zum Flughafen Tegel zu führen.

A western extension of the radial line E had already been planned when it first opened back in 1930, but the project only got underway after the fall of the Wall and in conjunction with the construction of the government district and a new central railway station. For financial reasons, however, construction work was temporarily halted, and the western section was only brought into service in 2009 as the U55 shuttle. The missing link between Brandenburger Tor and Alexanderplatz, the construction of which was fully resumed in 2012, may now be completed in 2019. Older plans included a further western extension of line U5 to Tegel Airport via Turmstraße (U9) and Jungfernheide (U7).

Erfahren Sie mehr über diese Linie in unserer Reihe:

Berliner U-Bahn-Linien: U5 - Von Ost nach West

von A. Seefeldt & R. Schwandl

Planung
Bau
Betrieb
Stationen

ISBN 978-3-936573-36-7
(Neuauflage Mai 2013)

U55 — Hauptbahnhof — 08-08-2009

Die ersten drei Stationen der Westverlängerung der U5 gingen 2009 als U55 in Betrieb. Bis zur Inbetriebnahme der Strecke zum Alexanderplatz findet nur ein Shuttle-Verkehr auf einem Gleis statt.

Der U-Bhf **Hauptbahnhof** liegt östlich neben dem Tiefbahnhof des im Mai 2006 eröffneten Berliner Hauptbahnhofs. Die weißen Emailplatten an den Wänden zieren Ansichten der ehemals zahlreichen Berliner Kopfbahnhöfe, z.B. des Frankfurter Bahnhofs (unten).

Mitten im Regierungsviertel liegt der U-Bhf **Bundestag**. In der großen Halle dominiert Sichtbeton, in Harmonie mit dem benachbarten Kanzleramt, das ebenfalls von den Architekten Axel Schultes und Charlotte Frank entworfen wurde.

Der U-Bhf **Brandenburger Tor** ist mit 17 m Tiefe der am tiefsten liegende im Berliner U-Bahn-Netz, seine Bahnsteighalle wurde durch Vereisung des Bodens aufgefahren. An den Wänden sind Schautafeln zur Geschichte dieses weltbekannten Stadttores angebracht (rechts).

Brandenburger Tor

The first three stations on the western extension of line U5 were brought into service as line U55 in 2009. Until the route to Alexanderplatz has been completed, a shuttle will continue operating on a single track.

The U-Bahn station **Hauptbahnhof** is located to the east of the underground portion of Berlin's Central Station, which opened in May 2006. The white enamelled panels on the walls depict views of Berlin's once numerous terminal stations, e.g. the Frankfurter Bahnhof (left).

In the middle of the government district lies **Bundestag** station. The large station hall is dominated by exposed concrete, in harmony with the adjacent Chancellery, which was also designed by the architects Axel Schultes and Charlotte Frank.

At 17 m below the surface, **Brandenburger Tor** station is the deepest on the Berlin underground network; its platform hall was excavated once the soil had been frozen. The walls feature panels illustrating the history of this famous city gate (above).

| 08-08-2009 | Bundestag | U55 |

| 08-08-2009 | Brandenburger Tor | U55 |

U5 — Unter den Linden ~2019

Visualisierung: bünck+fehse, Berlin

Die drei Stationen auf dem fehlenden Abschnitt zwischen Alexanderplatz und Brandenburger Tor sind seit 2012 nun auch für die Berliner Bevölkerung und die zahlreichen Besucher deutlich wahrnehmbar im Bau. Sie sollen nach derzeitiger Planung 2019 eröffnet werden.

An der Kreuzung Unter den Linden/Friedrichstraße entsteht ein Turmbahnhof in L-Form für die Linien U5 und U6, der den Namen **Unter den Linden** tragen wird, weshalb der frühere S-Bahnhof mit diesem Namen bereits zur Eröffnung des danebenliegenden U-Bahnhofs der U55 2009 auch den Namen „Brandenburger Tor" erhielt. Am neuen Umsteigebahnhof bekommt die U5 auf der unteren Ebene einen breiten Mittelbahnsteig mit getrennten Aufgängen zur U6, für die zwei Seitenbahnsteige gebaut werden. Der Gestaltungsentwurf stammt von Ingrid Hentschel – Prof. Axel Oestreich Architekten BDA, die auch für den benachbarten U-Bhf Brandenburger Tor verantwortlich zeichneten und dessen Ähnlichkeit mit seinem Schwarz-Weiß-Kontrast nicht zu übersehen ist.

Der U-Bhf **Museumsinsel** wird quer unter dem Kupfergraben neben der Schlossbrücke errichtet. Die Ausgänge werden beiderseits des nicht schiffbaren Kanals angeordnet, im Westen in der Straße Unter den Linden und im Osten auf dem zukünftigen Platz vor dem wiederaufzubauenden Berliner Schloss. Die unter Anwendung der chemischen Vereisung aufzufahrende Bahnsteighalle wurde von Max Dudler gestaltet, wobei neben den Steinplatten auf dem Boden und an den Wänden und Säulen der Sternenhimmel über dem Gleisbett auffällt.

Direkt vor dem **Berliner Rathaus** (auch bekannt als *Rotes Rathaus*) wird der gleichnamige U-Bahnhof liegen. Die Seitenbahnsteige der U5 werden sich hier in eineinhalbfacher Tieflage befinden. Darunter entsteht eine Aufstellanlage, die zu einem späteren Zeitpunkt zu einer Bahnsteigebene für eine meist als U3 bezeichnete Linie (Weißensee – Kurfürstendamm) ausgebaut werden könnte. Der Gestaltungsentwurf von CollignonArchitektur wurde mehrmals umgearbeitet, nicht zuletzt nachdem bei archäologischen Vorarbeiten die Fundamente eines mittelalterlichen Rathauses ans Tageslicht kamen.

The three stations on the missing section between Alexanderplatz and Brandenburger Tor have been fully under construction since 2012, something very noticeable to both Berliners and the city's numerous visitors. These stations are currently scheduled to be opened in 2019.

At the intersection Unter den Linden/Friedrichstraße, an L-shaped interchange station for lines U5 and U6 is being built. It will be called **Unter den Linden**, *which is why the former S-Bahn station of that name was already renamed Brandenburger Tor in 2009 when the adjacent U55 station opened. At the new interchange, line U5 will boast a wide island platform on the lower level with separate flights of stairs and elevators leading to line U6, for which two side platforms are being built. The station was designed by Ingrid Hentschel – Prof. Axel Oestreich Architekten BDA, who were also responsible for the neighbouring Brandenburger Tor station, and the similarity between the two with their black-and-white colour schemes is clearly evident.*

Museumsinsel *station lies next to Schlossbrücke, diagonally under the Kupfergraben, a non-navigable canal. The exits are placed on either side of the canal, to the west on the boulevard Unter den Linden, and to the east on what will become the main square in front of the Berliner Schloss (the old royal palace), which will be reconstructed from scratch in the near future. The station will be excavated using ground-freezing techniques. The interior design is by Max Dudler, and besides the stone slabs on the floor, walls and pillars, it features a starry sky over the track beds.*

The underground station **Berliner Rathaus** *will be located directly in front of its namesake, i.e the City Hall. The side platforms for line U5 will be on level -1.5. One level below, there will be an area with sidings which may later be converted into a platform level for what is usually referred to as line U3 (Weißensee – Kurfürstendamm). The station design, conceived by Collignon-Architektur, had to be modified several times, most recently after preliminary archaeological work uncovered the foundations of a medieval town hall.*

Museumsinsel — U5
~2019

Visualisierung: bünck+fehse, Berlin

Berliner Rathaus — U5
~2019

Visualisierung: bünck+fehse, Berlin

U5 — Alexanderplatz — 21-12-1930

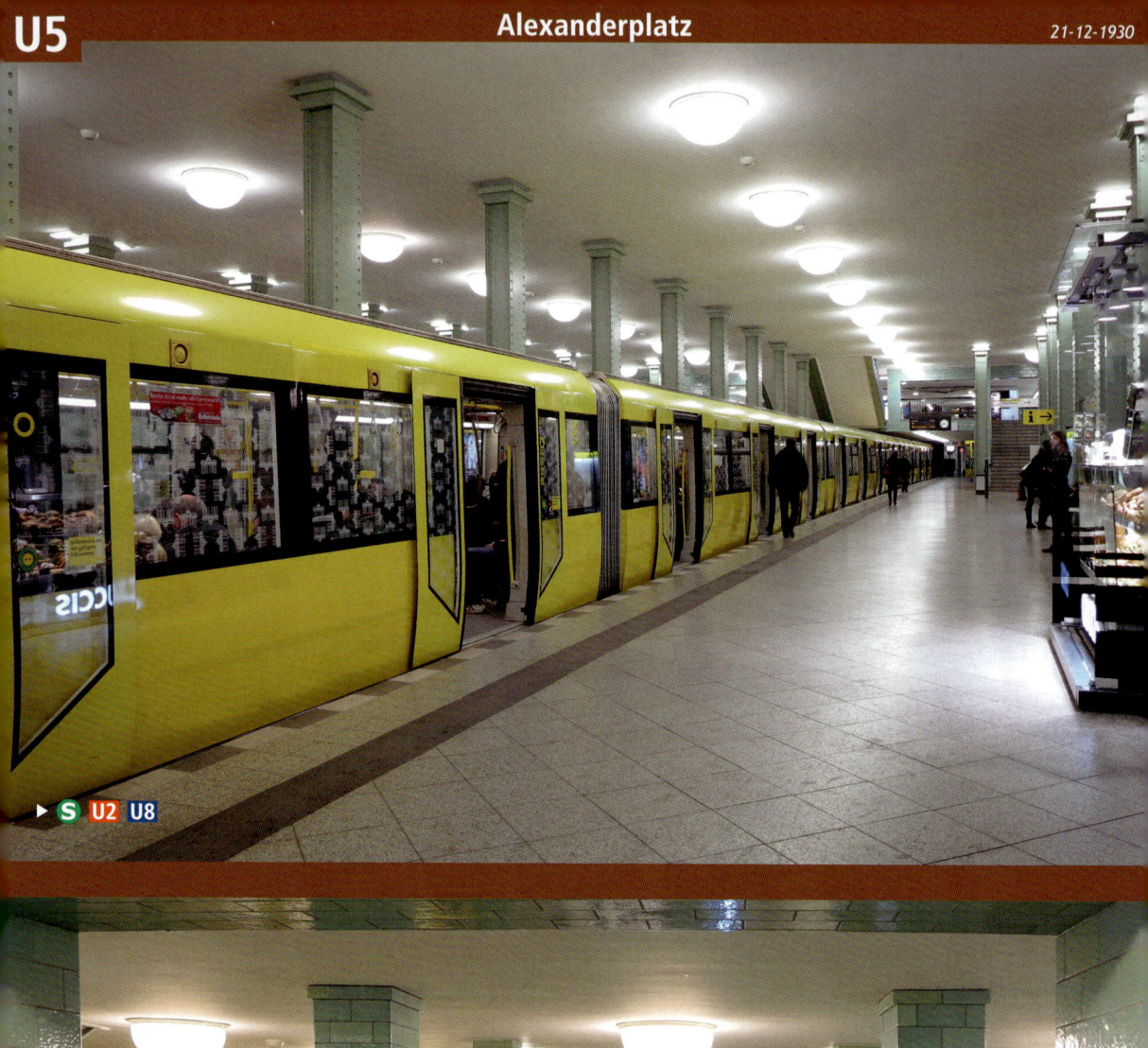

▶ S U2 U8

← U5 Hönow

60

Schillingstraße U5

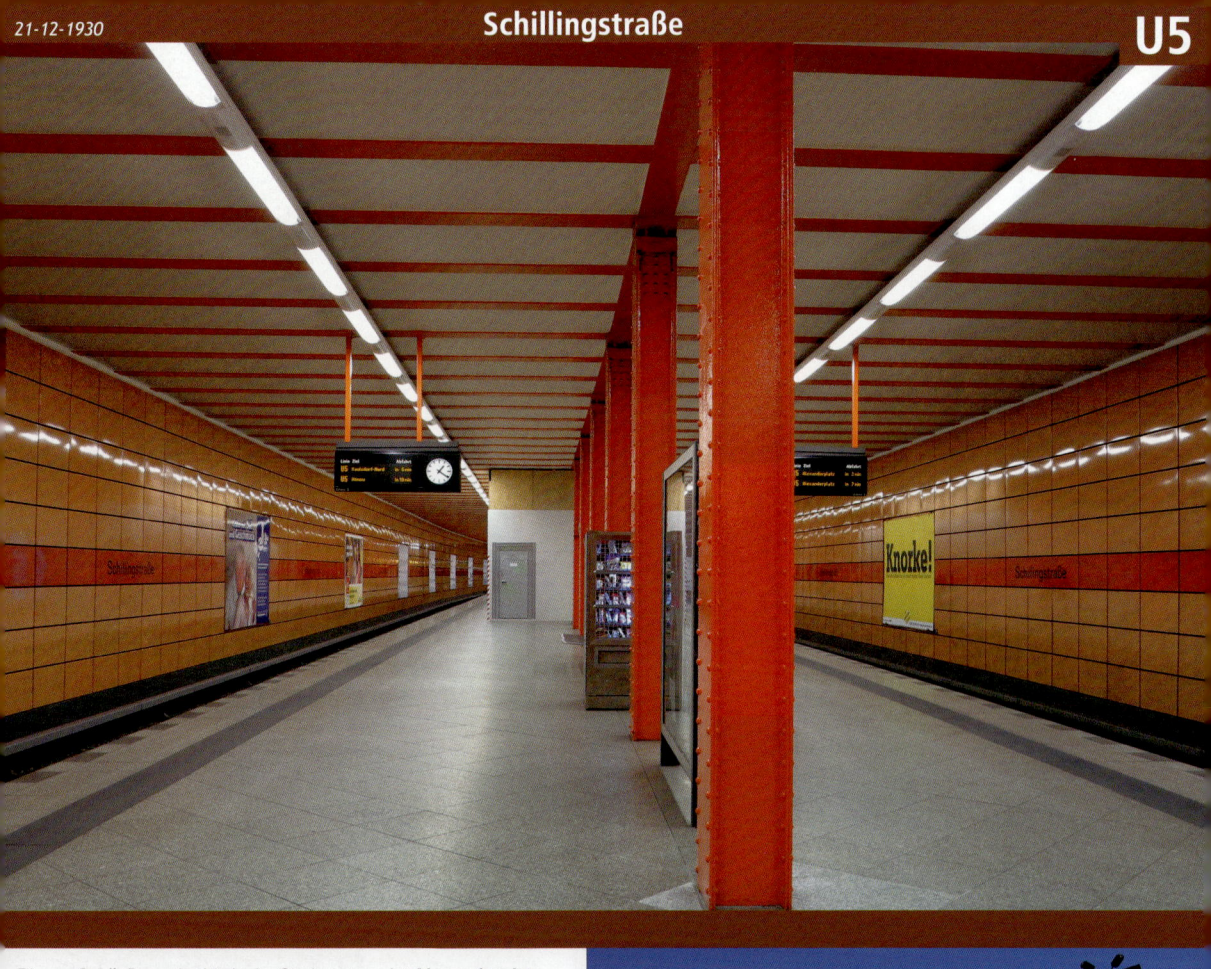

21-12-1930

Bis zur Schließung der Lücke im Stadtzentrum ist **Alexanderplatz** der westliche Endpunkt der heutigen U5. Hier treffen drei U-Bahn-Linien aufeinander, deren Bahnsteigebenen die Form eines H bilden. Die U5 hält dabei auf der untersten Ebene in 12,9 m Tiefe auf den beiden inneren Gleisen des viergleisigen Bahnhofsteils. Auf den äußeren Gleisen sollte einst eine Linie von Weißensee Richtung Kurfürstendamm verkehren. Die U5-Bahnsteigebene wurde in den Jahren 2003/04 vollständig modernisiert, wobei sich die Neuverfliesung an die ursprüngliche anlehnt. Die vormals schwarz gestrichenen Stützen passen nun farblich zu den Seitenwänden. Die Renovierung des östlichen Zugangsbereichs (unten) folgte 2008.

Der U-Bhf **Schillingstraße** wurde wie die folgenden Stationen während einer Streckensperrung im Jahr 2003 neu gestaltet. Dabei kamen an den Wänden Emailplatten zur Anwendung, die sich farblich an die ursprüngliche Verfliesung anlehnen, die jedoch in den 1960er Jahren ersetzt worden war. Das Eingangsgebäude am südöstlichen Zugang fügt sich architektonisch in die Umgebung ein (rechts).

Until the gap in the city centre is closed, **Alexanderplatz** will remain the western terminus of line U5. This station is an interchange for three U-Bahn lines, whose three platform levels form an H. Line U5 stops on the lowest level at a depth of 12.9 m, using the two inner tracks of the four-track station. The outer tracks were built for a line once planned to run from Weißensee to Kurfürstendamm. The U5 platform level was completely modernised in 2003/04 with new tiles just like the original ones. The previously black supports now match the colour of the walls. The renovation of the eastern entrance area (left) followed in 2008.

Along with the stations following it, **Schillingstraße** was completely refurbished during a partial line closure in 2003. The walls are now covered with enamelled panels, which in each station take on the colour scheme of the original tiling that was replaced in the 1960s. The entrance building at the southeast corner blends in architecturally with the surroundings (above).

Alexanderplatz

U5 Strausberger Platz 21-12-1930

2003 wurden auch die folgenden drei Stationen grundsaniert und dabei neu gestaltet. Sie liegen alle unter der ehemaligen Stalinallee, heute Karl-Marx-Allee, die durch ihren „Zuckerbäckerstil" der 1950er Jahre bekannt ist. Am U-Bhf **Strausberger Platz** ist der südwestliche Zugang (wie am Frankfurter Tor der südöstliche) in ein Gebäude integriert (rechts).

Wie Samariterstraße oder Magdalenenstraße gehört der U-Bhf **Weberwiese** zum Normaltyp der alten Linie E, der einen Mittelbahnsteig in eineinhalbfacher Tiefenlage mit Zwischengeschossen an beiden Enden aufweist.

Auch wenn das namensgebende Stadttor näher am U-Bhf Weberwiese lag, bilden die beiden Türme über dem U-Bhf **Frankfurter Tor** seit den 1950er Jahren eine Art Tor zur Karl-Marx-Allee. Kein anderer Bahnhof wurde in Berlin so oft umbenannt (siehe Anhang). Einst als Kreuzungsbahnhof mit der U1 konzipiert, ist hier die Bahnsteighalle sehr niedrig ausgefallen. Der mittige Ausgang zur Straßenbahn kam 2008 hinzu (unten).

In 2003, the next three stations were also fully refurbished and redesigned. They all lie under the former Stalinallee, now Karl-Marx-Allee, which is known for its Socialist Classicism style of the 1950s. At **Strausberger Platz** station, the southwestern access (like the southeastern at Frankfurter Tor) is integrated into an adjacent building (right).

Like Samariterstraße and Magdalenenstraße stations, **Weberwiese** belongs to the standard line E type, which features an island platform on level -1.5 and mezzanines at both ends.

Although the eponymous city gate lay closer to Weberwiese station, the two towers above **Frankfurter Tor** station have represented a sort of gateway to Karl-Marx-Allee since the 1950s. No other station in Berlin has been renamed so often (see Annex). Once planned to become an interchange with line U1, the platform area features a rather low ceiling. The central exit that leads to the tram stop was only added in 2008 (left).

62

21-12-1930 **Weberwiese** **U5**

21-12-1930 **Frankfurter Tor** **U5**

63

U5 Samariterstraße 21-12-1930

Da die ursprüngliche Wandverfliesung im U-Bhf **Samariterstraße** in den 1970er Jahren nicht verändert wurde und sich noch immer in einem guten Zustand befand, wurde dieser Bahnhof unter Denkmalschutz gestellt und bei der Sanierung der Strecke 2003 ausgeklammert. Einzig die vormals rot gestrichenen Stützen erstrahlen nun in Hellgrün. Der Denkmalschutz erlaubte es leider nicht, den traditionellen Asphaltboden durch elegantere Granitplatten zu ersetzen, ein Aufzug konnte jedoch auch hier 2012 eingebaut werden.

Als Umsteigepunkt zum S-Bahn-Ring trug der U-Bhf **Frankfurter Allee** zeitweise den Zusatz *Ringbahn*. Umsteigende Fahrgäste müssen allerdings einen kurzen Fußweg entlang der Ringbahntrasse zurücklegen, während das benachbarte Einkaufszentrum über einen direkten Zugang zum U-Bahnhof verfügt.

Mitte der 1980er Jahre wurde der U-Bhf **Magdalenenstraße** erstmals umgestaltet. Dabei wurden Wandmalereien, die sich auf die deutsche Geschichte des 20. Jahrhunderts beziehen, angebracht. Bei der Modernisierung 2003 wurden diese in die neue Gestaltung integriert.

Frankfurter Allee

Since the original tiles in **Samariterstraße** station had not been replaced in the 1970s and had survived in good condition, the station became a listed monument and was thus excluded from the 2003 rehabilitation of the line, although the supports were changed from previously red to light green to match the tiles. Unfortunately, the heritage office did not allow the traditional asphalt floor to be replaced by more elegant granite plates, although permission was granted to add a lift in 2012.

As a transfer station to the S-Bahn ring line, **Frankfurter Allee** station at times carried the appendage 'Ringbahn'. Transferring passengers, however, need to walk a short distance at the surface, while the adjacent shopping centre is directly accessible from the U-Bahn station.

Magdalenenstraße station was first refurbished in the mid-1980s. The walls were then enhanced with artwork depicting scenes from 20th century German history. In the modernisation carried out in 2003, these images were integrated into the new design.

21-12-1930 Frankfurter Allee U5

21-12-1930 Magdalenenstraße U5

65

U5 — Lichtenberg — 21-12-1930

Zu DDR-Zeiten hatte sich der Bahnhof Lichtenberg zu einem wichtigen Fernbahnhof entwickelt, heute fahren hier Regionalbahnen ins nordöstliche Umland ab. Der U-Bhf **Lichtenberg** liegt quer unter den Gleisen der S- und Fernbahn, ein nur 2,25 m hohes Zwischengeschoss dient als Übergang (s. Seite 54). Die ursprüngliche gelbe Wandverfliesung war bis 2003 erhalten.

43 Jahre lang war der U-Bhf **Friedrichsfelde** die Endstation der Linie E. Ähnlich den älteren Berliner U-Bahnhöfen liegt der Mittelbahnsteig direkt unter der Straßenoberfläche und ist über Treppen an beiden Enden zugänglich. Die ursprüngliche blaugrüne Wandverfliesung war bis 2003 teilweise erhalten.

Tierpark ist die einzige unterirdische Station, die im ehemaligen Ost-Berlin errichtet wurde. Der Blick durch die großzügige Bahnsteighalle wird durch ein mittig eingehängtes Abfertigerhäuschen eingeschränkt. Am U-Bhf Tierpark kann man ohne Überqueren von Straßen zu den Tram-Linien M17, 27 und 37 umsteigen. Ein Wandmosaik ziert das nördliche Zwischengeschoss (unten).

In the GDR, **Lichtenberg** used to be a major railway station, but today it is only the departure point for some regional trains towards the northeast of Brandenburg. The U-Bahn station Lichtenberg is located diagonally under the S-Bahn and mainline tracks, and is separated from them by a mezzanine just 2.25 m high (see p. 54). The original yellow wall tiling remained intact until the 2003 modernisation.

For 43 years, **Friedrichsfelde** was the terminus of line E. Rather like the older Berlin underground stations, the island platform is located directly below the road surface and is accessible via stairs at both ends. Some of the original blue-green tiles survived until 2003.

Tierpark was the only underground station built in the former East Berlin. The view through the large station is restricted by a raised dispatcher's office in the middle. At Tierpark, transfer to tram lines M17, 27 and 37 is provided without the need to cross any streets. A wall mosaic embellishes the northern mezzanine (left).

Tierpark

21-12-1930 **Friedrichsfelde** **U5**

25-06-1973 **Tierpark** **U5**

67

U5 — Biesdorf-Süd — 01-07-1988

Ab Biesdorf-Süd liegen alle U-Bahnhöfe der U5 an der Oberfläche. Der ebenerdige U-Bhf **Biesdorf-Süd** verfügt über drei Gleise, hier endeten früher einzelne Verstärkerfahrten. Der Mittelbahnsteig ist über eine Unterführung erreichbar, der stadteinwärtige Seitenbahnsteig von der Nordseite her ebenerdig. Gestalterisch sind die 1988/89 errichteten Stationen eher unauffällig, wobei man bei genauem Hinschauen erkennen kann, dass die Stützen und Dachausleger jeweils in einer anderen Farbe gestrichen sind. Der Zugangsbereich ist in der Regel mit roten Backsteinen verkleidet und verfügt über eine Rampe, was diese Stationen von Anfang an behindertenfreundlich machte.

Der U-Bhf **Elsterwerdaer Platz** liegt auf einem Damm, hier beeindruckt die lange, überdachte Rampenanlage (rechts).

Der Bahnhof **Wuhletal** verfügt über zwei Mittelbahnsteige, wobei an den jeweils äußeren Kanten die S-Bahn (S5) hält, so dass man hier bequem zwischen U- und S-Bahn umsteigen kann. In diesem Bereich gibt es auch eine Gleisverbindung zwischen den beiden Schnellbahnnetzen.

Elsterwerdaer Platz

From **Biesdorf-Süd** onwards, all the U5 stations lie on the surface. The ground-level station Biesdorf-Süd has three tracks as it used to function as the terminus for some peak-hour trains. While the island platform is accessible via an underpass, the inbound side platform can also be reached at grade from the northern side. The 1988/89 stations are rather inconspicuous, although a closer look reveals that the roof supports and beams are painted a different colour in each of them. The access area is generally covered with red bricks and has a ramp, which made these stations fully accessible from the start.

Elsterwerdaer Platz station lies on an embankment and features a long covered ramp (above).

Wuhletal station has two island platforms, with the respective outer edges used by S-Bahn line S5, thus providing convenient transfer between U-Bahn and S-Bahn. In this area, there is also a track connection between the two rapid transit networks.

Wuhletal

01-07-1988 **Elsterwerdaer Platz** U5

01-07-1989 **Wuhletal** U5

Kaulsdorf-Nord

U5 — 01-07-1989

Nach einem 1,1 km langen Tunnel erreicht die U5 den U-Bhf **Kaulsdorf-Nord**, wo tagsüber außerhalb der Hauptverkehrszeiten jeder zweite Zug endet. Der Bahnhof liegt in einem Einschnitt, eingebettet in ein Stadtteilzentrum einer Großsiedlung aus den 1980er Jahren. Um Graffiti keine Chance zu geben, wurden die Wände vor einigen Jahren mit Szenen aus der U-Bahn bemalt.

Wenig attraktiv und meist mit zerschlagenen Scheiben präsentiert sich der im Einschnitt gelegene U-Bhf **Neue Grottkauer Straße**. Mehrere Stationen dieser Neubaustrecke trugen bei ihrer Eröffnung im Juli 1989, also wenige Monate vor dem Fall der Berliner Mauer, Namen von ehemaligen DDR-Politikern, die jedoch 1991 verschwanden (siehe Anhang).

Der U-Bhf **Cottbusser Platz** liegt ebenerdig und ist über eine Unterführung mit Rampe (rechts) und Treppe zum Mittelbahnsteig erreichbar. Der südliche Ausgang mündet in einen Park, der sich parallel zur U-Bahn-Strecke bis zur Endstation erstreckt.

Cottbusser Platz

After a 1.1 km tunnel, line U5 reaches **Kaulsdorf-Nord**, where every other train terminates during daytime off-peak service. The station is located in a cutting and embedded in the town centre of the 1980s housing estate. To prevent unauthorised graffiti, the walls were painted with scenes from the U-Bahn a few years ago.

The rather unattractive **Neue Grottkauer Straße** station, located in a cutting, is conspicuous for its broken window panes. Several stations on this extension carried the names of East German politicians when the line opened in July 1989, i.e. a few months before the collapse of the Berlin Wall, but these names disappeared in 1991 (see Annex).

Cottbusser Platz station lies at ground level and is accessible via an underpass, from where a ramp (above) and stairs lead up to the island platform. The southern exit leads to a park, which extends parallel to the U-Bahn line all the way to the terminus.

01-07-1989 **Neue Grottkauer Straße** **U5**

01-07-1989 **Cottbusser Platz** **U5**

71

U5 — Hellersdorf — 01-07-1989

Am im Einschnitt gelegenen U-Bhf **Hellersdorf** kann man ohne Überqueren von Straßen zu den Tram-Linien M6 und 18 umsteigen. Dadurch ergibt sich ein längerer Tunnel zwischen den Gleisen am westlichen Bahnhofsende, wo vor einigen Jahren Wandbilder mit Graffiti-Technik entstanden (unten).

Bis zur Anpassung der Ländergrenzen im Jahr 1991 lag der im weiten Einschnitt gelegene U-Bhf **Louis-Lewin-Straße** wie der Endbahnhof Hönow außerhalb der Berliner Stadtgrenzen. Er ist wie Hellersdorf von Brücken an beiden Bahnhofsenden zugänglich.

Mit 58 m über dem Meeresspiegel ist der Endbahnhof **Hönow** die höchstgelegene Station im Berliner U-Bahn-Netz. Der dreigleisige Bahnhof ist von der Ostseite ebenerdig zugänglich (die Stadtgrenze verläuft direkt vor dem Eingang), an der Westseite führt eine eingehauste Brücke über die Gleise. Der südliche Seitenbahnsteig ist nicht überdacht, denn dieses Gleis dient normalerweise nur als Abstellmöglichkeit für Züge.

Hellersdorf station lies in a wide trench and provides transfer to tram lines M6 and 18 without any streets having to be crossed. This is achieved by means of a long tunnel between the tracks at the western end of the platform, where the walls were adorned with graffiti art a few years ago (left).

Until the border between Berlin and the State of Brandenburg was modified in 1991, the last two stations on line U5 lay outside the city boundaries. **Louis-Lewin-Straße** station also lies in the trench, and like Hellersdorf, it is accessible from a bridge at either end of the station.

At 58 m above sea level, the terminus **Hönow** is the highest station on the Berlin U-Bahn network. The three-track station is accessible at grade from the eastern side (with the city border running right outside the entrance), while on the western side an encased bridge spans the tracks. The southern side platform is not covered because that track is normally only used for stabling trains.

01-07-1989 **Louis-Lewin-Straße** **U5**

01-07-1989 **Hönow** **U5**

73

U6 — Alt-Tegel – Alt-Mariendorf

Friedrichstraße

Die heutige Linie U6 wurde 1923 als „Nordsüdbahn" unter der zentralen Friedrichstraße in Betrieb genommen. Es handelte sich dabei nicht nur um die erste von der Stadt Berlin selbst errichtete Strecke, sondern auch um die erste Großprofilstrecke: Statt der bislang nur 2,30 m breiten Züge sollten fortan 2,65 m breite eingesetzt werden. Allerdings baute man anfangs im Gegenzug kürzere Bahnsteige, die nur vier Wagen der später eingesetzten Typen aufnehmen konnten, so dass in den 1990er Jahren alle Bahnhöfe im Stadtzentrum für den Einsatz der üblichen 6-Wagen-Züge verlängert werden mussten.

Die ursprüngliche Strecke, die bald die Bezeichnung „Linie C" bekam, wurde mit zwei Streckenästen nach Süden verlängert, einem nach Tempelhof und einem zweiten Richtung Neukölln, der später in der neuen U7 aufging. Bereits 1966, nun als „Linie 6", erreichte die U6 ihre heutige Ausdehnung.

Today's line U6 opened in 1923 as the 'Nordsüdbahn' (north-south line), which ran underground through the city centre along Friedrichstraße. This was not only the first line the City of Berlin built by itself, but also the first large-profile line on the network: instead of the previously just 2.30 m wide cars, now 2.65 m ones were used. In return, platforms were initially shorter and could only accommodate four cars of the later types, so in the 1990s all the underground stations in the city centre had to be extended to allow the common 6-car trains to be used.

The original route, which soon became 'line C', was extended south with two branches, one to Tempelhof and another to Neukölln, the latter eventually being integrated into the new U7. By 1966, then labelled 'Linie 6', line U6 had reached its current length.

U6

19.9 km (2.9 km oberirdisch | *surface*)
29 Bahnhöfe | *stations*

30-01-1923: Hallesches Tor – Naturkundemuseum
08-03-1923: Naturkundemuseum – Seestraße
19-04-1924: Hallesches Tor – Mehringdamm [– Gneisenaustraße]
14-02-1926: Mehringdamm – Platz der Luftbrücke
10-09-1927: Platz der Luftbrücke – Paradestraße
22-12-1929: Paradestraße – Tempelhof
03-05-1956: Seestraße – Kurt-Schumacher-Platz
31-05-1958: Kurt-Schumacher-Platz – Alt-Tegel
13-08-1961: [X] Schwartzkopffstraße, Zinnowitzer Straße, Oranienburger Tor, Französische Straße, Stadtmitte
28-02-1966: Tempelhof – Alt-Mariendorf
01-07-1990: +* Schwartzkopffstraße, Zinnowitzer Straße, Oranienburger Tor, Französische Straße, Stadtmitte
~2019: [X] Französische Straße, + Unter den Linden

[X] Schließung | *Closure*   * Wiederinbetriebnahme | *Reopening*

Scharnweberstraße > Otisstraße (Autobahn A111)

Das einschneidendste Ereignis in der Geschichte der U6 war sicherlich der Bau der Berliner Mauer am 13. August 1961, als plötzlich alle U-Bahnhöfe der U6 im zum sowjetischen Sektor gehörenden Bezirk Mitte (Schwartzkopffstraße bis Stadtmitte) geschlossen wurden. Die Züge der West-Berliner U-Bahn durchfuhren diese Geisterbahnhöfe bis 1990 ohne Halt. Eine Ausnahme bildete der U-Bahnhof Friedrichstraße, wo auf Ost-Berliner Gebiet innerhalb des West-Berliner Netzes zur Nord-Süd-S-Bahn sowie zur Stadtbahn Richtung Westen umgestiegen werden konnte. Außerdem fungierte der Bahnhof Friedrichstraße als wichtiger Grenzübergang zwischen den beiden Stadthälften.

Seit Juli 2012 und bis Ende 2013 ist die U6 im Stadtzentrum unterbrochen, um den Bau des Umsteigebahnhofs Unter den Linden (U5/U6) zu ermöglichen, der ca. 2019 eröffnet wird.

The most dramatic event in the history of line U6 was certainly the erection of the Berlin Wall on 13 August 1961, when all the U6 underground stations located in the district of Mitte, which lay in the Soviet sector, were suddenly closed (Schwartzkopffstraße to Stadtmitte). Until 1990, West Berlin U-Bahn trains used to run through these ghost stations without stopping. The only exception was Friedrichstraße station, where it was possible to change between West Berlin trains (the U6, north-south S-Bahn and westbound Stadtbahn) in East Berlin territory. In addition, Friedrichstraße station was an important border crossing between East and West Berlin.

Through service on line U6 was interrupted in the city centre in July 2012 to allow for the construction of the interchange station Unter den Linden (U5/U6), now scheduled to open in 2019. Full service on line U6 will resume in late 2013.

Französische Straße

Erfahren Sie mehr über diese Linie in unserer Reihe:

Berliner U-Bahn-Linien: U6 - Die "Nordsüdbahn" durch Mitte

von Alexander Seefeldt

Planung
Bau
Betrieb
Stationen

ISBN 978-3-936573-34-3

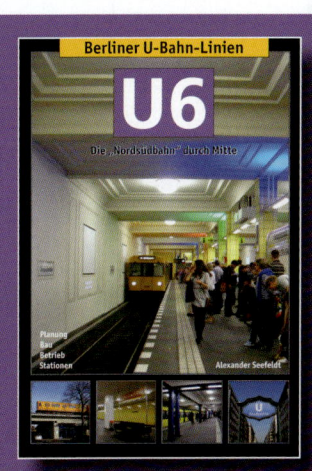

U6 — Alt-Tegel
31-05-1958

Die nördlichsten Stationen der U6 haben sich in den letzten 10 Jahren kaum verändert. Die Endstation **Alt-Tegel** sowie der U-Bhf **Borsigwerke** weisen den typischen Stil der 1950er Jahre auf, der auch auf der U9 zu finden ist, mit einer hellen Wandverfliesung in einer jeweils unterschiedlichen Farbe sowie der sogenannten Schmetterlingsdecke. Im U-Bhf Borsigwerke ist bis heute das originale Bahnsteigmobiliar mitsamt den roten Schildern erhalten. Während diese Station noch nicht behindertengerecht zugänglich ist, wurde im U-Bhf Alt-Tegel 2006 ein Aufzug eingebaut.

Neben der U5 ist die U6 die einzige Großprofillinie mit einem oberirdischen Abschnitt. Auf dieser fast 3 km langen Strecke liegen drei weitgehend baugleiche, seitlich offene Stationen in Dammlage, die wie am Bahnhof **Holzhauser Straße** von einer durchgehenden Überdachung aus Stahlbeton dominiert werden. Farbliche Akzente an den Bahnsteigaufbauten und Eingängen (hier türkis und rot) bringen etwas Abwechslung hinein.

The northernmost stations on line U6 have hardly changed in the last ten years. The terminus at *Alt-Tegel* as well as *Borsigwerke* station are in the typical 1950s style also found on line U9: each station's walls are tiled in a different pale colour, and there is a so-called 'butterfly' ceiling. Borsigwerke station preserves the original platform furniture, including the red signs. While this station is not yet fully accessible, a lift was added at Alt-Tegel in 2006.

Besides line U5, U6 is the only large-profile line with a surface section. On this almost 3 km long segment there are three nearly identical stations: they lie on an embankment and are open on both sides. Like at *Holzhauser Straße*, they are dominated by a continuous canopy of reinforced concrete. Colour accents on the platform structures and entrances (here in turquoise and red) add some variety.

Borsigwerke

31-05-1958 — **Borsigwerke** — U6

31-05-1958 — **Holzhauser Straße** — U6

U6 — Otisstraße — 31-05-1958

Inmitten von Kleingärten gelegen, gehört der U-Bhf **Otisstraße** (vormals Seidelstraße) zu den weniger stark frequentierten Stationen der Berliner U-Bahn. Einst trug er den Zusatz „Flughafen Tegel", da vor Inbetriebnahme des heutigen Flughafens Tegel im Jahr 1974 der damalige französische Militärflughafen am Nordrand des Flugfelds auch für zivile Flüge genutzt wurde.

An der letzten oberirdischen Station **Scharnweberstraße** wurden rote Farbakzente gesetzt (rechts). Aufgrund des vorerst weiterhin bestehenden Flughafens Tegel liegt das Einzugsgebiet dieses U-Bahnhofs nur nordöstlich der Station. Wie am U-Bhf Otisstraße wurde hier 2010 ein Aufzug nachgerüstet.

Die erste U-Bahn-Verlängerung nach dem 2. Weltkrieg endete anfangs am U-Bhf **Kurt-Schumacher-Platz**, der von runden Säulen aus Naturstein geprägt wird. Rauchschürzen zieren seit einigen Jahren die in Bahnsteigmitte gelegenen Aufgänge (unten). Der südliche Stationsbereich wurde 1989 mit einem Einkaufszentrum überbaut. Die sandfarbenen Fliesen werden derzeit durch größere ersetzt.

Schwarnweberstraß

Surrounded by allotments, **Otisstraße** (formerly Seidelstraße) is one of the quieter stations on the Berlin U-Bahn system. It once had the appendage 'Flughafen Tegel', as before today's airport opened at Tegel in 1974, the former French military airport on the northern edge of the airfield was also used for civilian flights.

At the last above-ground station, **Scharnweberstraße**, the distinguishing colour is red (above). Due to the still operating Tegel Airport, this station's catchment area lies just to the northeast. Like at Otisstraße, a lift was retrofitted here in 2010.

The first U-Bahn extension after World War II initially reached **Kurt-Schumacher-Platz**, a station characterised by round columns of natural stone. For several years, smoke curtains have embraced the staircases located in the middle of the platform (left). In 1989, a shopping centre was built over the southern part of the station. The sand-coloured tiles are currently being replaced with larger ones.

31-05-1958 **Scharnweberstraße** **U6**

03-05-1956 **Kurt-Schumacher-Platz** **U6**

U6 — Afrikanische Straße

03-05-1956

Die beiden ersten Stationen der Nordverlängerung der U6 aus den 1950er Jahren wurden 2012 modernisiert. Beide gehören wie Alt-Tegel und Borsigwerke zum Standardtyp dieser Zeit, wobei der U-Bhf **Afrikanische Straße**, der früher an den Seitenwänden den Zusatz „Friedrich-Ebert-Siedlung" trug, die Kennfarbe Hellblau und der U-Bhf **Rehberge** die Kennfarbe Lindgrün erhielt. Während bei ersterem die typischen sechseckigen Stützen mit buntem Glasmosaik verkleidet sind, gibt es bei letzterem eine gelbe Terrazzoverkleidung. Auch wenn die neuen Fliesen größer sind, so wurde doch der Farbton weitgehend beibehalten. Rehberge erstrahlt außerdem bereits mit einem neuen Granitboden und einem markanten Aufzugsgebäude (unten).

Die ursprüngliche nördliche Endstation der „Nordsüdbahn", **Seestraße**, wurde im Laufe der Geschichte mehrmals umgebaut. Heute verfügt die dreigleisige Anlage über einen Mittelbahnsteig und einen Seitenbahnsteig direkt unter der Straßenoberfläche und ohne Verbindungstunnel. Das mittlere Gleis wird für Fahrten vom und zum Betriebshof genutzt. Die gelbe Wandverfliesung stammt von 1955, als die Strecke nach Tegel verlängert wurde.

The first two stations on the 1950s northern extension were refurbished in 2012. Like Alt-Tegel and Borsigwerke, both are of the standard type of this period. **Afrikanische Straße**, which used to show the appendage 'Friedrich-Ebert-Siedlung' on its side walls, is light blue and **Rehberge** lime green. While the typical hexagonal columns in the former station are clad in glass mosaic tiles, the latter has a yellow terrazzo finish. Although larger, the new tiles almost match the original colour. Rehberge station also features a new granite floor and a distinctive lift pavilion (left).

Seestraße, the original northern terminus of the 'Nordsüdbahn', has been rebuilt several times during its history. Today, the three-track station has an island platform and a side platform located directly below the road surface, and without a connecting tunnel. The centre track is used by trains to and from the depot. The yellow tiled walls are from 1955, when the route was extended to Tegel.

Rehberge

03-05-1956 **Rehberge** U6

08-03-1923 **Seestraße** U6

U6 — Leopoldplatz — 08-03-1923

▶ U9

Der U-Bahnhof **Leopoldplatz** hatte ursprünglich einen Mittelbahnsteig und eine weinrote Verfliesung der Seitenwände. Er wurde 1960 im Zuge des Baus der U9 komplett umgebaut. Die vormals in sattem BVG-Gelb gestrichenen Stützen erscheinen seit einigen Jahren in einem etwas blassen Grün (unten).

Die meisten U-Bahnhöfe der ursprünglichen „Nordsüdbahn" hatten keine Wandverkleidung. Diese bekam der U-Bhf **Wedding** im Zuge einer Bahnsteigverlängerung Anfang der 1970er Jahre. Die vormals dunkelblau gestrichenen Stützen sind seit 2002 grau, womit sie mit dem damals verlegten Granitboden harmonieren. Der südliche Ausgang (rechts) fungiert als Übergang zur Ringbahn.

Der U-Bhf **Reinickendorfer Straße**, der letzte im ehem. West-Berlin, gehört zum Standardtyp der „Nordsüdbahn", mit einer jeweils unterschiedlich gestalteten Decke, gestrichenen Wänden und einer kräftigen Kennfarbe an Stützen und Deckenträgern. Allerdings hatte der Architekt Alfred Grenander hier ursprünglich Weiß vorgesehen.

Wedd

Leopoldplatz

Leopoldplatz station originally had an island platform and its side walls were tiled in burgundy. It was completely rebuilt in 1960 in conjunction with the construction of line U9. For some years now, the supports previously painted in a saturated BVG yellow have been coated in a somewhat pale green (left).

Most of the original 'Nordsüdbahn' underground stations had no wall cladding. At **Wedding**, tiles were added in the early 1970s when the platform was extended. The previously dark-blue supports were painted grey in 2002 to match the new granite floor. The southern entrance (above) provides transfer to the Ringbahn.

Reinickendorfer Straße station was the last stop in the former West Berlin. It belongs to the standard 'Nordsüdbahn' type: each station has a different ceiling structure, painted walls, and a strong distinguishing colour on supports and cross beams. The architect Alfred Grenander, however, had originally assigned the colour white to this station.

Wedding U6

Reinickendorfer Straße U6

U6 Schwartzkopffstraße 08-03-1923

Die nächsten drei U-Bahnhöfe wurden von 1961 bis 1990 durch die Teilung Berlins zu Geisterbahnhöfen. Kurioserweise wurde der damals bereits 12 Jahre zugemauerte U-Bhf „Walter-Ulbricht-Stadion" 1973 von der DDR-Regierung in „Stadion der Weltjugend" umbenannt, seit 1991 heißt er wieder wie ursprünglich **Schwartzkopffstraße**. Wie bei den folgenden Stationen wurde Anfang der 1990er Jahre der Mittelbahnsteig verlängert. Ursprünglich hatten die meisten Stationen der „Nordsüdbahn" an jedem Bahnsteigende zwei hintereinanderliegende Treppen. Eine davon wich nun in der Regel dem neuen Aufzug. Die Straßenbahn fuhr hier 2013 noch über der U-Bahn (unten).

Im Rahmen seiner dritten Umbenennung wurde der U-Bhf **Naturkundemuseum** 2009 mit Bildern aus dem namensgebenden Museum anstelle der sonst üblichen Werbetafeln neu gestaltet. Ein lebensgroßes Saurierskelett ziert den südlichen Zugang (rechts).

Im U-Bhf **Oranienburger Tor** mit der Kennfarbe Blau wird die Decke statt wie sonst von Einzelstützen von Doppelstützen getragen.

Naturkundemuseum

Between 1961 and 1990, when the city was divided into two parts, the following three stations became ghost stations. Although it had been sealed off for 12 years, **Schwartzkopffstraße** station was renamed from 'Walter-Ulbricht-Stadion' to 'Stadion der Weltjugend' in 1973, before regaining its original name in 1991. Like at the next two stations, the island platform was extended in the 1990s. Originally, most of the stations had two sets of stairs at each end of the platform, located one behind the other. One of these exits was now replaced with a lift. In 2013, the tram still ran on top of the U-Bahn tunnel at this point (left).

Along with its third renaming, **Naturkundemuseum** station was enhanced in 2009, with images from the eponymous museum replacing the usual advertising posters. A life-size dinosaur skeleton adorns the southern entrance (above).

At **Oranienburger Tor** with its blue colour scheme, twin supports instead of single ones carry the ceiling.

30-01-1923 **Naturkundemuseum** **U6**

30-01-1923 **Oranienburger Tor** **U6**

U6 Friedrichstraße 30-01-1923

Der U-Bhf **Friedrichstraße** blieb als einziger der U6 auf dem Ost-Berliner Abschnitt auch während der Teilung Berlins quasi als exterritoriale Umsteigestation sowie als Grenzübergang geöffnet. Während der vorübergehenden Sperrung des Abschnitts Friedrichstraße – Französische Straße 2012/13 zum Bau des Umsteigebahnhofs Unter den Linden verkehren auf dem Nordabschnitt der U6 nur 4-Wagen-Züge, dadurch konnte die sonst sehr schmale Treppe am südlichen Bahnsteigende provisorisch erweitert werden (unten).

Ca. 2019 wird der U-Bhf **Französische Straße** mit seiner grünen Kennfarbe endgültig geschlossen und durch den neuen U-Bhf Unter den Linden ersetzt. Da dies bereits bei der Bahnsteigverlängerung Anfang der 1990er Jahre so vorgesehen war, wurde hier kein Aufzug eingebaut, stattdessen stehen hier weiterhin an beiden Enden die hintereinander angeordneten Treppen in Straßenmitte zur Verfügung (rechts). Die Bahnsteighalle als solches soll erhalten bleiben, auch wenn die Art einer späteren Nutzung derzeit noch unklar ist.

Friedrichstraße was the only U6 station in East Berlin territory to remain in service during the division of Berlin, because it functioned as an extraterritorial interchange station and border crossing. During the temporary closure of the section Friedrichstraße – Französische Straße in 2012/13 due to the construction of the Unter den Linden interchange, the northern section of line U6 is only being served by 4-car trains, which allowed the very narrow staircase at the southern end of the platform to be temporarily widened (left).

In around 2019, *Französische Straße* station with its green colour scheme will be closed permanently and replaced by the new interchange station Unter den Linden. Since this had already been envisaged when the platform was extended in the early 1990s, no lift was installed here, and instead, the original entrance/exit arrangement with two staggered stairways in the middle of the road is still available (above). The platform area is to be preserved, although its future function is yet to be determined.

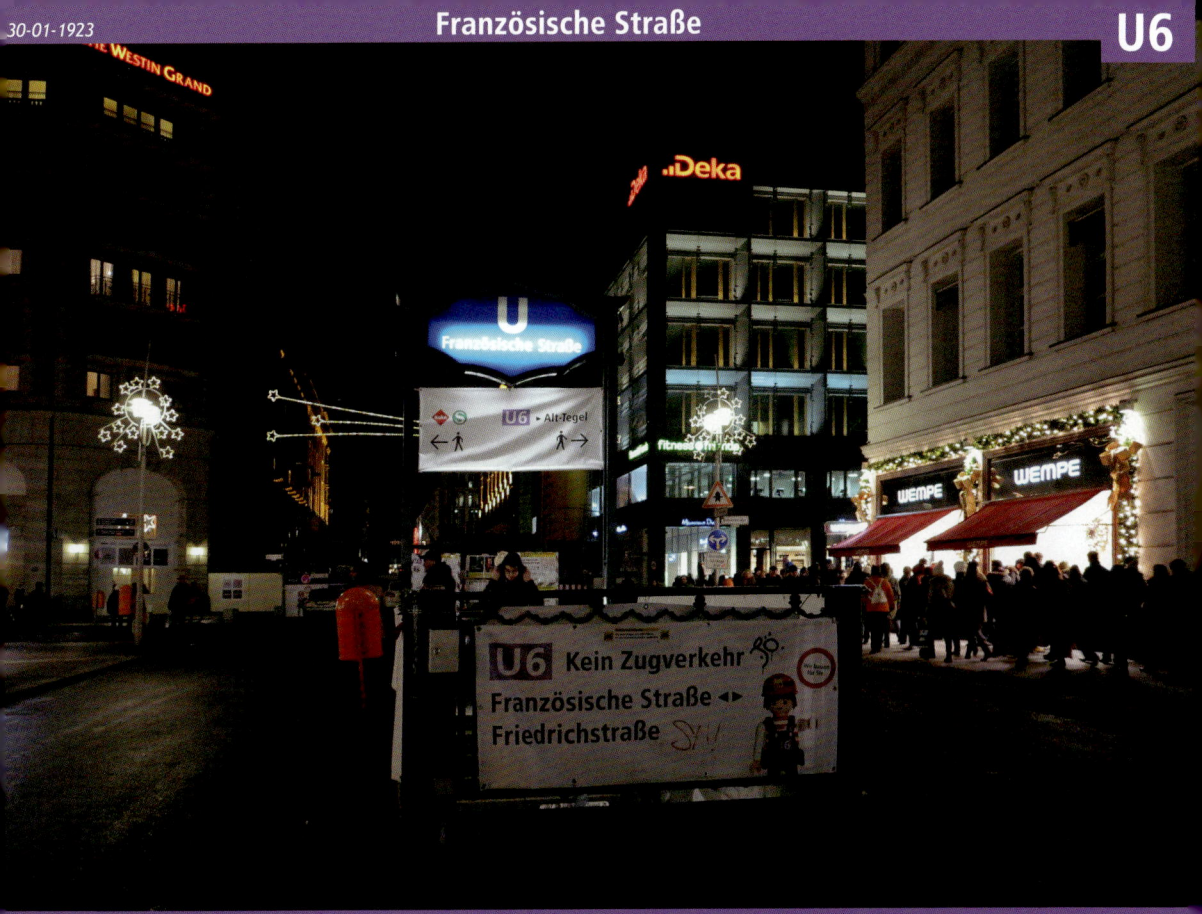

Französische Straße U6

30-01-1923

U6

Stadtmitte

U6 — 30-01-1923

▶ U2

Der U-Bhf **Stadtmitte** war der letzte Geisterbahnhof, bevor die Züge der U6 auf ihrer Fahrt Richtung Süden wieder West-Berlin erreichten. Zur U2 gelangt man über den 160 m langen sog. „Mäusetunnel", eine für Berliner Verhältnisse unbequeme Umsteigeverbindung (rechts).

Direkt südlich der einstigen Berliner Mauer liegt der U-Bhf **Kochstraße**, der seit 1995 auf den Schildern als Hinweis für die zahlreichen Touristen den Zusatz „Checkpoint Charlie" trägt.

Am U-Bhf **Hallesches Tor** endete die ursprüngliche „Nordsüdbahn". Wegen der südlich anschließenden Unterfahrung des Landwehrkanals liegt der Bahnsteig tiefer als bei den vorangegangenen Stationen. Daraus und durch die Konkurrenz zur einst privaten Hochbahn ergab sich ein langer Umsteigetunnel zur heutigen U1. Dieser wurde im Jahr 2012 neu gestaltet (unten). Die Wandverkleidung mit blauen Eternitplatten auf der Bahnsteigebene stammt von Mitte der 1970er Jahre, als der Bahnsteig für 6-Wagen-Züge verlängert wurde. Der Einbau eines Aufzugs ist geplant.

Stadtmitte

Stadtmitte station was the last ghost station before southbound U6 trains returned to West Berlin. The U2 station is connected via the 160 m 'mouse tunnel', by Berlin standards a rather inconvenient transfer option (above).

Kochstraße station is located just south of the former Berlin Wall, and since 1995 the signs have been appended with 'Checkpoint Charlie' to help tourists find their way.

Hallesches Tor was the original southern terminus of the 'Nordsüdbahn'. Due to the crossing under the Landwehrkanal just south of the station, the platform lies deeper than in the previous stations. For this reason and because of the competition with the once private 'Hochbahn', the connecting tunnel that leads to the U1 station is rather long; it was refurbished in 2012 (left). The blue panels of asbestos cement at platform level are from the mid-1970s, when the platform was extended to accommodate 6-car trains. A lift is planned.

Hallesches Tor

88

| 30-01-1923 | Kochstraße | U6 |

| 30-01-1923 | Hallesches Tor | U6 |

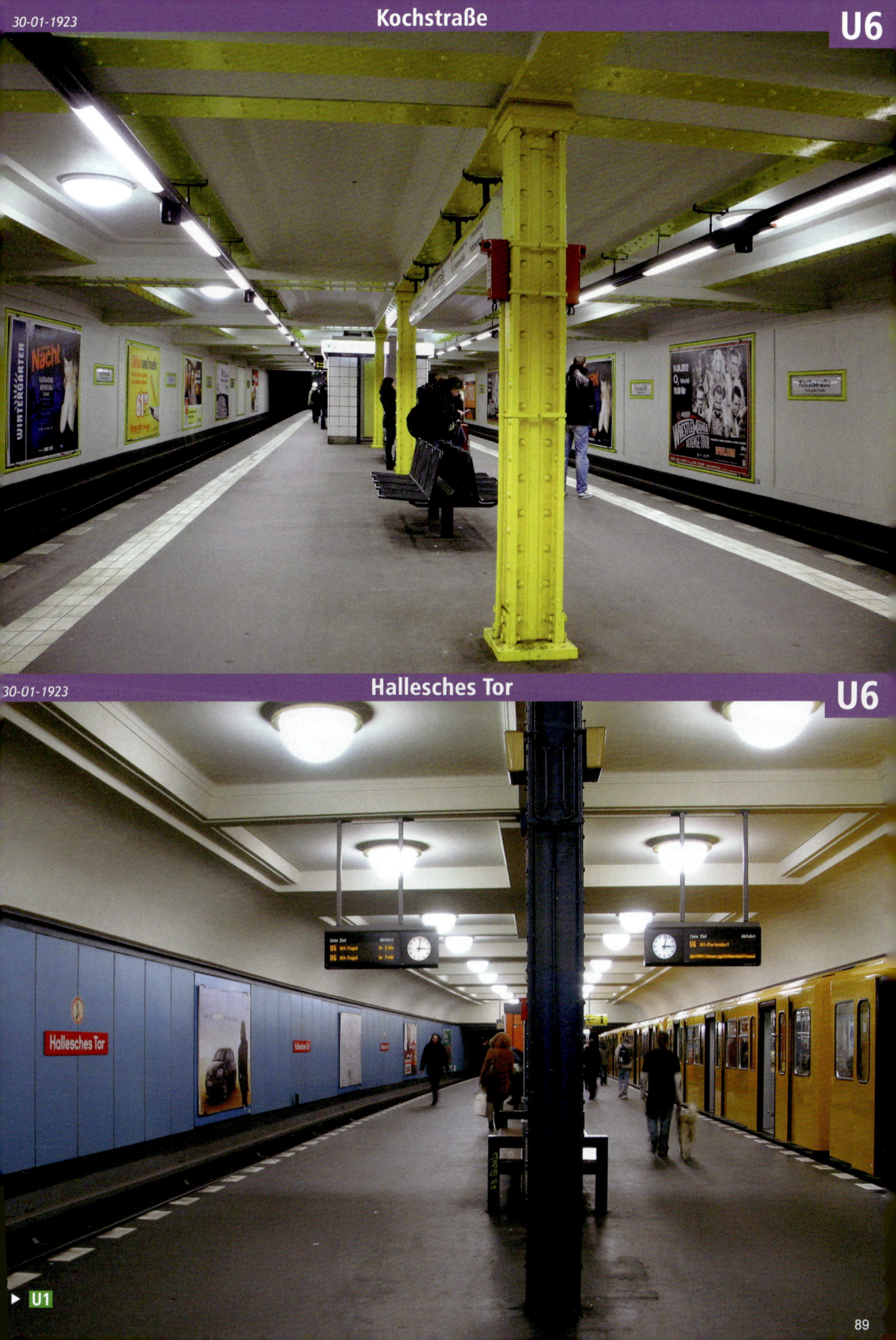

U6 — Mehringdamm — 19-04-1924

▶ U7

Der U-Bhf **Mehringdamm** ging 1924 in Hinblick auf eine Streckenverzweigung als dreigleisiger Bahnhof in Betrieb. In Vorbereitung auf die Linientrennung im Zuge der Schaffung der U7 wurde der U-Bahnhof Mitte der 1960er Jahre an der Westseite um ein Gleis erweitert und komplett umgestaltet, wobei die gewölbte Decke verschwand. Diese wurde nun bei einer Modernisierung 2011/12 weitgehend wiederhergestellt, während die Seitenwände statt der ursprünglich verputzten Wände nun großflächige graubraune Fliesen erhielten.

Der U-Bhf **Platz der Luftbrücke**, unweit des 2008 geschlossenen Flughafens Tempelhof, erstrahlt weiterhin ohne Mittelstützen in seiner klassischen, von Alfred Grenander geschaffenen Form.

Anfangs diente der heutige U-Bhf **Paradestraße** als Zugang zum Flughafen Tempelhof, derzeit ist er nur von der Westseite des Tempelhofer Damms bzw. seit 1990 auch über einen direkten Aufzug erreichbar. 1990 wurden die grau glasierten Wandfliesen nach einer Idee von Gabriele Stirl durch eine farbige Komposition ersetzt.

Platz der Luftbrück[e]

Mehringdamm opened in 1924 as a three-track station in provision for a future branch to Tempelhof, while the main route continued to Neukölln. The junction was completely rebuilt in the mid-1960s in preparation for the creation of the separate U7: a fourth track was added on the western side and the original vaults were hidden behind a false ceiling. The vaults were restored in a modernisation project in 2011/12, when the side walls, originally plastered, were clad with large grey-brown tiles.

Platz der Luftbrücke station, located close to Tempelhof Airport, which has been out of service since 2008, still boasts an elegant design by Alfred Grenander without the otherwise common central pillars.

In the beginning, **Paradestraße** station functioned as a gateway to the airport, but now it is only accessible via entrances on the western side of Tempelhofer Damm, or since 1990, a direct lift from the surface to the platform. In 1990, the original grey glazed tiles were replaced with a colourful pattern designed by Gabriele Stirl.

14-02-1926 **Platz der Luftbrücke** **U6**

10-09-1927 **Paradestraße** **U6**

U6 — Tempelhof — 22-12-1929

Der U-Bhf **Tempelhof**, dessen Zusatz „Südring" auf die Umsteigemöglichkeit zur S-Bahn hinweist, war 37 Jahre lang südlicher Endpunkt des Tempelhofer Astes der Linie C. In der weitgehend original erhaltenen, großzügig angelegten Bahnsteighalle setzt das in den 1980er Jahren angebrachte geometrische Muster an der Decke, das auf das Rollfeld am Flughafen anspielt, einen besonderen Akzent.

Der U-Bhf **Alt-Tempelhof** war der letzte, der von Bruno Grimmek entworfen wurde, der seit den 1950er Jahren für die Gestaltung aller neuen Stationen verantwortlich war.

Grimmeks Nachfolger Rainer G. Rümmler entwickelte erst nach und nach seinen eigenen Stil, weshalb der U-Bhf **Kaiserin-Augusta-Straße** dem nördlichen Nachbarn stark ähnelte. Allerdings fielen hier die Fliesen bald ab und die Wand wurde einfach dunkelgrün gestrichen. Auch wenn die Renovierungsarbeiten (Entfernung der abgehängten Decke, neuer Granitboden, Aufzugeinbau) bereits vor ca. 5 Jahren begannen, sind die Wände auch 2013 noch sehr unansehnlich.

Alt-Tempelhof

At **Tempelhof**, the appendage 'Südring' indicates the possibility of transferring to the S-Bahn ring line. For 37 years, the station used to be the southern terminus of line C's Tempelhof branch. It is mostly preserved in its original style, although the geometrical pattern painted on the ceiling in the 1980s as an allusion to the nearby airport runway adds a special note.

Alt-Tempelhof was the last station designed by Bruno Grimmek, who had been responsible for all the U-Bahn stations built since the 1950s.

Grimmek's successor, Rainer G. Rümmler, only gradually developed his own style, and accordingly, **Kaiserin-Augusta-Straße** station initially looked rather similar to the previous one. But the tiles soon fell off the walls, which were then simply painted dark green. Although a station refurbishment programme (including a new granite floor, a retrofitted lift and the removal of the false ceiling) has been going on for some five years, the side walls are still in a rather pitiful state in 2013.

Kaiserin-Augusta-Straße

28-02-1966 **Alt-Tempelhof** **U6**

28-02-1966 **Kaiserin-Augusta-Straße** **U6**

93

U6   Ullsteinstraße   28-02-1966

Im U-Bhf **Ullsteinstraße** reichte eine neue Bahnsteigbeleuchtung aus, um ca. 2005 aus einem einst eher schummrigen Bahnhof eine freundliche Station zu machen. Der U-Bahnhof liegt nicht unter der Erde, sondern eingebaut in die Straßenbrücke über den Teltowkanal.

Statt einer völligen Neugestaltung wurden die dunkelblauen Wände im U-Bhf **Westphalweg** 2009 mit weißen Flächen und darauf angebrachten Blumenmotiven verschönert. Bemerkenswert ist außerdem, dass die beiden nördlichen Zugänge in die Bebauung integriert sind (rechts), was in Berlin eher selten ist.

Der südliche Endpunkt der U6, **Alt-Mariendorf**, ist ein wichtiger Umsteigepunkt zu zahlreichen Buslinien. Aufgrund des starken Fahrgastaufkommens erhielt er am südlichen Bahnsteigende eine doppelte Treppen- bzw. Fahrtreppenanlage. Neben den von Anfang an vorhandenen weißen Wandfliesen und den roten und blauen kleinteiligen Fliesen an den Treppenumwehrungen wurden 2009 auch die Stützsäulen weinrot verkleidet.

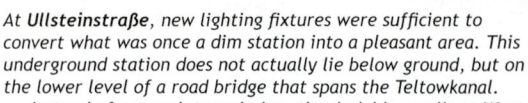

At **Ullsteinstraße**, new lighting fixtures were sufficient to convert what was once a dim station into a pleasant area. This underground station does not actually lie below ground, but on the lower level of a road bridge that spans the Teltowkanal.

Instead of a complete redesign, the dark blue walls at **Westphalweg** station were interposed with white areas filled with different flower motifs. The two northern entrances to the station are integrated into adjacent buildings, a rather uncommon feature on the Berlin U-Bahn system.

The busy southern U6 terminus **Alt-Mariendorf** offers interchange between the U-Bahn and many connecting bus lines. To cope with this heavy passenger load, there are two staggered staircases, including up and down escalators, at the southern end of the station. From the beginning, the side walls have been clad in white tiles and the staircases in red and blue mosaics, but the centre pillars were only covered with burgundy tiles in 2009.

| 28-02-1966 | Westphalweg | U6 |
| 28-02-1966 | Alt-Mariendorf | U6 |

U7 — Rathaus Spandau – Rudow

Bayerischer Platz

Die U7 ist Berlins längste U-Bahn-Linie, eine der schnellsten und, auch wenn einige Stationen bereits aus den 1920er Jahren stammen, die neueste Linie. Wie die U9 verkehrt sie ausschließlich auf dem Gebiet des ehemaligen West-Berlin und verbindet die alten Bezirke Spandau, Charlottenburg, Wilmersdorf, Schöneberg, Kreuzberg und Neukölln. Sie berührt dabei aber nicht das West-Berliner Zentrum rund um den Bahnhof Zoo, sondern fungiert als schnelle Querverbindung, teils parallel zur Ringbahn.

Der älteste Abschnitt zwischen Mehringdamm und Grenzallee entstand bereits in den 1920er Jahren als Neuköllner Ast der „Nordsüdbahn", der ehemaligen Linie C und heutigen U6. 1966 wurde dieser Ast abgekoppelt und die als Linie H geplante Linie 7 gebildet, die in mehreren Etappen in beide Richtungen verlängert wurde, bis schließlich 1984 die heutige U7 vollendet war.

Line U7 is the longest, one of the fastest, as well as the newest metro line in Berlin despite the fact that some stations date back to the 1920s. Running exclusively in former West Berlin territory like line U9, it links the old districts of Spandau, Charlottenburg, Wilmersdorf, Schöneberg, Kreuzberg and Neukölln. It also avoids the centre of West Berlin around Zoo Station, and instead functions as a fast tangential connection, running in part parallel to the S-Bahn ring line.

The oldest section, which lies between Mehringdamm and Grenzallee, was built in the 1920s as the Neukölln branch of the 'Nordsüdbahn', the former line C and today's U6. In 1966, this branch was detached, and though planned as line H, it became line 7. It was extended in both directions in several stages, reaching its present form in 1984.

U7

31.8 km (gänzlich unterirdisch | *completely underground*)
40 Bahnhöfe | *stations*

19-04-1924: Mehringdamm – Gneisenaustraße*
14-12-1924: Gneisenaustraße – Südstern*
11-04-1926: Südstern – Karl-Marx-Straße*
21-12-1930: Karl-Marx-Straße – Grenzallee*
28-09-1963: Grenzallee – Britz-Süd*
28-02-1966: Mehringdamm – Möckernbrücke
02-01-1970: Britz-Süd – Zwickauer Damm
29-01-1971: Möckernbrücke – Fehrbelliner Platz
01-07-1972: Zwickauer Damm – Rudow
28-04-1978: Fehrbelliner Platz – Richard-Wagner-Platz
01-10-1980: Richard-Wagner-Platz – Rohrdamm
01-10-1984: Rohrdamm – Rathaus Spandau

* als Ast der Linie C (U6) | *as a branch of line C (U6)*

Adenauerplatz

...hrbelliner Platz

Durch die lange Entstehungsgeschichte weist die U7 eine entsprechende Vielfalt bei der Bahnhofsgestaltung auf. Mitte der 1960er Jahre ging die Verantwortung dafür von Bruno Grimmek auf Rainer G. Rümmler über, dessen kreative Produktivität auf dem Spandauer Abschnitt der U7 (z. B. Paulsternstraße) ihren Höhepunkt erreichte.

Von Rathaus Spandau sollte die U7 ursprünglich um vier Stationen bis zur Heerstraße in Staaken verlängert werden. Von Rudow ist eine Erweiterung bis zum alten Flughafen Schönefeld möglich, beim Bau des neuen Flughafens wurden diesbezüglich keine Vorleistungen getroffen. An mehreren Bahnhöfen der heutigen U7 gibt es erhebliche Bauvorleistungen, um in Zukunft das Umsteigen zu weiteren Linien so einfach wie möglich zu gestalten: Rathaus Spandau, Jungfernheide, Adenauerplatz, Kleistpark.

Because of its long history, line U7 offers a great variety of station designs. In the mid-1960s, this responsibility was handed over from Bruno Grimmek to Rainer G. Rümmler whose creative productivity reached its peak on the Spandau section of line U7 (e.g. Paulsternstraße).

From Rathaus Spandau, line U7 was to be extended by four stations to Heerstraße in Staaken. From Rudow, an extension to the old Schönefeld Airport is possible, although in the construction of the new airport, an extension to the future terminal was not taken into account. At several stations on today's U7, significant provisions were made to allow easy interchange with other lines in the future, namely at Rathaus Spandau, Jungfernheide, Adenauerplatz and Kleistpark.

Erfahren Sie mehr über diese Linie in unserer Reihe:

Berliner U-Bahn-Linien: U7 – Quer durch den Westen

von A. Seefeldt & R. Schwandl

Planung · Bau
Betrieb · Stationen

ISBN 978-3-936573-37-4
(erscheint im Herbst 2013)

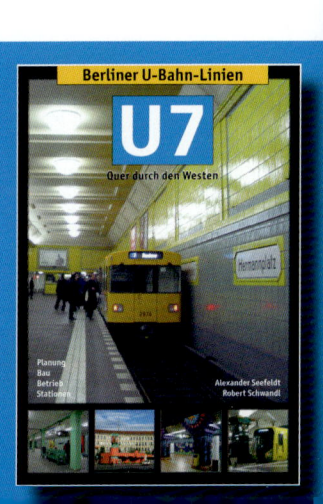

U7 — Rathaus Spandau

01-10-1984

Der westliche Endpunkt der U7, **Rathaus Spandau**, wurde großzügig als Umsteigestation zur U2 ausgelegt, die aus Ruhleben hierher verlängert werden sollte. Die äußeren Gleiströge liegen nun seit 1984 ungenutzt im abgesperrten Bereich. Ansonsten gilt der U-Bahnhof mit seinen mächtigen Säulen und laternenartigen Leuchtkörpern als eine der Kathedralen der Berliner U-Bahn.

Für Berlin sehr ungewöhnlich liegt der U-Bhf **Altstadt Spandau** unter der Bebauung. Er wurde in Caisson-Bauweise errichtet, wofür während der Bauzeit einige Häuser abgerissen und später wieder aufgebaut werden mussten. Durch die westlich anschließenden Röhrentunnel ergab sich ein breiter Bahnsteig mit doppelter Stützenreihe.

Der folgende U-Bahnhof **Zitadelle** liegt zwar etwa 350 m von der namensgebenden Spandauer Festung entfernt, dennoch spiegelt sich die Architektur der Verteidigungsanlage in der Gestaltung der Station, deren Wände mit Backsteinen verblendet sind, wider. Hier handelt es sich um den einzigen U7-Bahnhof mit Seitenbahnsteigen. An den Wänden sind u.a. historische Stadtpläne von Spandau zu sehen.

Zitadell

The western U7 terminus **Rathaus Spandau** was spaciously laid out to provide for future interchange with line U2, which was to be extended here from Ruhleben. The outer track beds have remained empty in the fenced-off area since 1984. With its massive columns and lantern-like lamps, this underground station is considered one of the Berlin U-Bahn's 'cathedrals'.

Altstadt Spandau station lies deep beneath some buildings, which is rather unusual for Berlin. It was built using caissons, so several houses had to be demolished during construction and later rebuilt. Due to the adjoining tube tunnels on the western side, the island platform is rather wide and has a double row of columns.

Zitadelle station is located some 350 m from the eponymous Spandau fortress, whose architecture is reflected in the red-brick design of the station. This is the only U7 station with side platforms. Among other images, historical maps of Spandau are mounted on the walls.

Rathaus Spandau

01-10-1984 — **Altstadt Spandau** — **U7**

01-10-1984 — **Zitadelle** — **U7**

U7 — Haselhorst — 01-10-1984

Im Vergleich zu manch anderem Bahnhof auf der Spandauer Strecke präsentiert sich der U-Bhf **Haselhorst** eher schlicht, doch verleihen die bis an die Decke auskragenden Aluminiumpaneele sowie die blaubraunen Keramikplatten an den Hintergleiswänden auch dieser Station eine gewisse Eleganz. Den nordöstlichen Ausgang erreicht man über einen langen Tunnel unter der nördlichen Fahrbahn der Nonnendammallee.

Ein Höhepunkt des Schaffens von Rainer G. Rümmler war sicherlich der U-Bhf **Paulsternstraße**, wo er inmitten des heutigen Industrie- und Gewerbegebiets eine längst verschwundene Naturlandschaft im späten Flower-Power-Stil wiederauferstehen ließ. Selbst die Decke wurde als Sternenhimmel in die Gestaltung einbezogen. Die mit Emailblechen verkleideten Stützen stellen Bäume dar, deren Baumwipfel in den Nachthimmel ragen. Zugänge zu dieser Station findet man nur an der Südseite der Nonnendammallee.

Haselhorst

Compared to other stations on line U7's Spandau section, **Haselhorst** appears rather simple, but with its cantilevered aluminium panels that reach the ceiling and blue-brown ceramic slabs on the walls, it also has a certain elegance. The northeastern exit is reached via a long tunnel under the westbound road lanes of Nonnendammallee.

One of the highlights of Rainer G. Rümmler's designs is certainly **Paulsternstraße** station. In the middle of an industrial and commercial zone, he recreated an idyllic landscape in late flower-power style. Even the ceiling with its starry sky became part of the design. The enamelled plates that clad the columns represent trees, the tops of which protrude into the night sky. Entrances to this station can only be found on the south side of Nonnendammallee.

01-10-1984　　Paulsternstraße　　U7

U7 — Rohrdamm — 01-10-1980

Der U-Bhf **Rohrdamm** liegt im Spandauer Stadtteil Siemensstadt, auch heute noch wichtiger Produktionsstandort des weltbekannten Konzerns. Inspiriert von diesem industriellen Umfeld wurden die Hintergleiswände mit stilisierten Zahnrädern, Kolben usw. geschmückt. Über dem Bahnsteig trägt eine Rohrsystem-Konstruktion das Leuchtband.

Der Erbauer der weltweit ersten elektrischen Straßenbahn sowie geistige Vater von Berlins erster U-Bahn-Strecke, Werner von Siemens, ist im Namen des U-Bhf **Siemensdamm** verewigt, den runde Wandtafeln mit Motiven aus den verschiedenen Bereichen des Industrieriesen schmücken. Bei einer Sanierung 2002/03 verschwanden allerdings schraubenschlüsselförmige Elemente, die die einzelnen Tafeln miteinander verbanden. Die früher grauen Wände wurden dabei grün gestrichen.

Ganz in Orange präsentierte sich bislang der U-Bhf **Halemweg**, dessen Ausgang in Bahnsteigmitte liegt und ohne Zwischengeschoss in einen Eingangspavillon mündet. Die Hintergleiswandverkleidung aus Holzpaneelen soll demnächst ersetzt werden.

Siemensdamm

Rohrdamm station is located in the Spandau neighbourhood of Siemensstadt, which is still an important production site for the world-famous industrial holding. Inspired by this environment, the walls behind the tracks were decorated with stylised gears, pistons, etc. Above the platform, a tubular structure carries a row of lamps.

The inventor of the world's first electric tram and father of Berlin's first U-Bahn line, Werner von Siemens, is immortalised in the name of **Siemensdamm** station, which is decorated with round wall panels depicting themes related to the various activities of the industrial giant. During renovations in 2002/03, however, the spanner-shaped elements that had linked the individual panels disappeared, while the previously grey walls were painted green.

The completely orange **Halemweg** station lies just below street level, with stairs and escalators leading from the middle of the platform to an entrance pavilion. The wooden wall panelling is soon to be replaced.

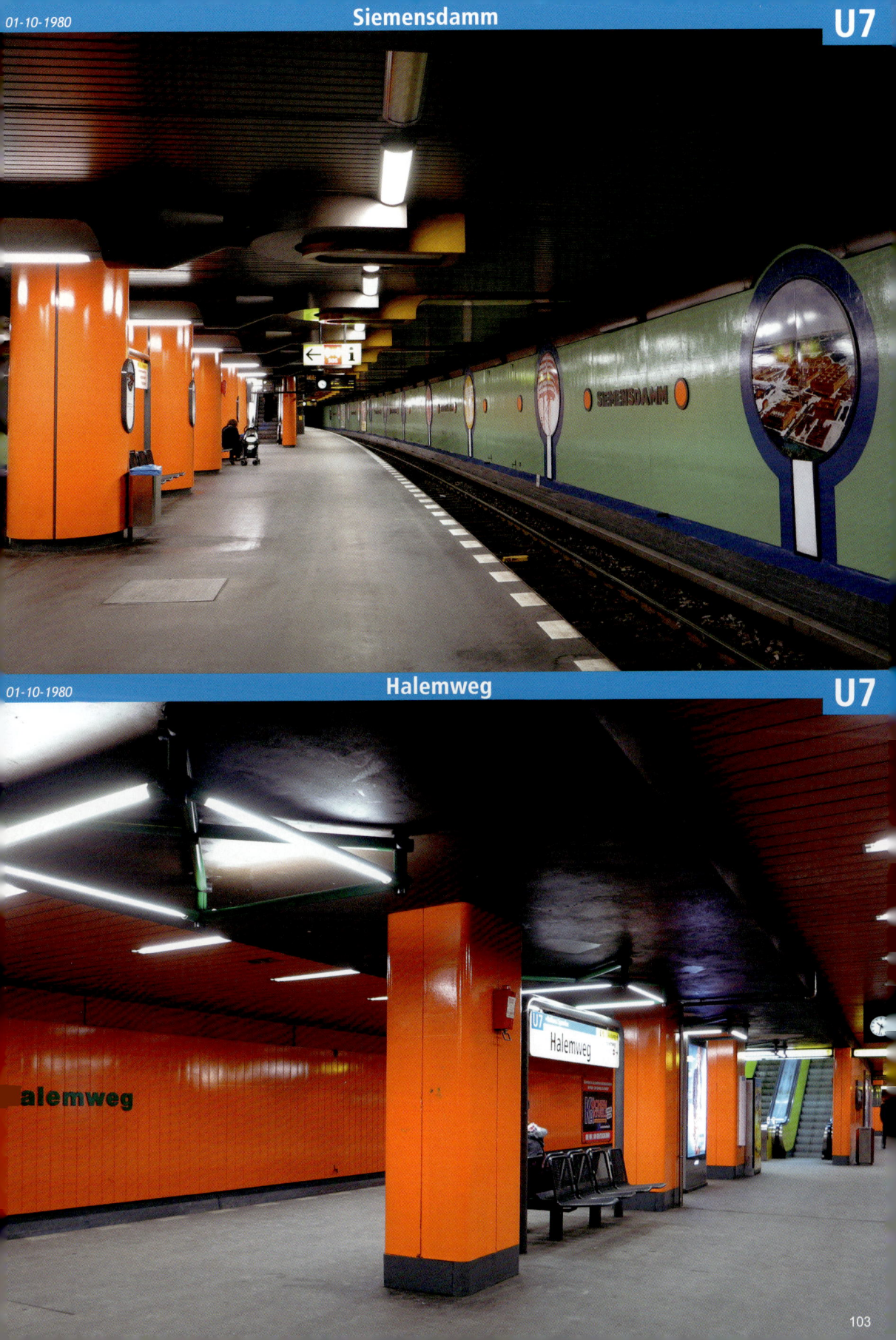

Siemensdamm
01-10-1980 — U7

Halemweg
01-10-1980 — U7

Jakob-Kaiser-Platz

U7 · 01-10-1980

Der U-Bhf **Jakob-Kaiser-Platz** wird derzeit umgestaltet: Die früheren Holzspanplatten an den Wänden und die Lamellen an der Decke wurden aus Brandschutzgründen entfernt. Außerdem wurde bereits ein Granitfußboden verlegt. Aufgrund der verspäteten Inbetriebnahme des neuen Flughafens BER steigen hier auch weiterhin zahlreiche Reisende in die Busse zum Flughafen Tegel um.

Der U-Bhf **Jungfernheide** wurde in den 1970er Jahren vorsorglich für zwei U-Bahn-Linien gebaut, denn hier sollte man eines Tages bequem von der U7 in die U5 Richtung Flughafen Tegel umsteigen können. Die U7 benutzt deshalb jeweils nur die westliche Bahnsteigkante des doppelstöckigen U-Bahnhofs (Richtung Rudow auf der oberen Ebene). Die Bahnsteige sind über hintereinander angeordnete Treppenanlagen direkt am südlichen Ende zugänglich, aber auch mittig miteinander über eine separate Treppe verbunden.

Der U-Bhf **Mierendorffplatz** liegt diagonal unter dem gleichnamigen Platz mit Zugängen an beiden Bahnsteigenden. Gestalterisch gehört er wie Jungfernheide zur verspielten Phase von R. G. Rümmler.

Jakob-Kaiser-Platz station is being refurbished in 2012/13, with the old chipboard panels on the walls and slats on the ceiling having been removed for reasons of fire safety. In addition, a granite floor was laid. Due to the delayed opening of the new airport BER, many travellers continue to change here to one of the buses to Tegel Airport.

Jungfernheide station was built in the 1970s in provision for two metro lines, so as to allow interchange between line U7 and line U5 towards Tegel Airport. Line U7 therefore only uses the western platform edges in the bi-level underground station, with Rudow-bound trains stopping on the upper level. The platforms are directly accessible at the southern end via staggered sets of stairs, but are also connected by a separate staircase located in the centre of the station.

Mierendorffplatz station lies diagonally under the eponymous square with entrances at either end of the platform. Like Jungfernheide, it belongs to Rainer G. Rümmler's whimsical creative period.

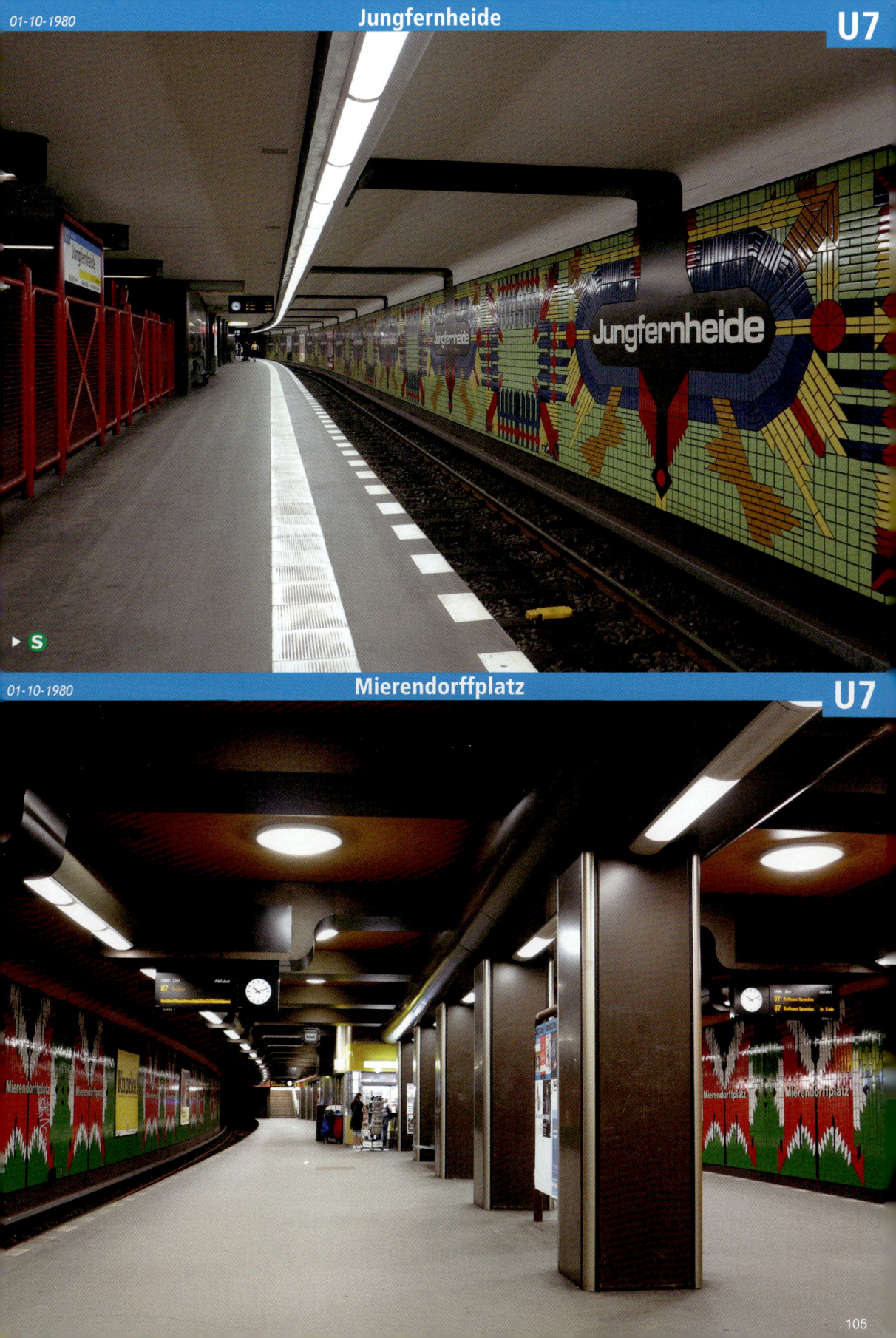

01-10-1980 | **Jungfernheide** | **U7**

01-10-1980 | **Mierendorffplatz** | **U7**

105

U7 — Richard-Wagner-Platz — 28-04-1978

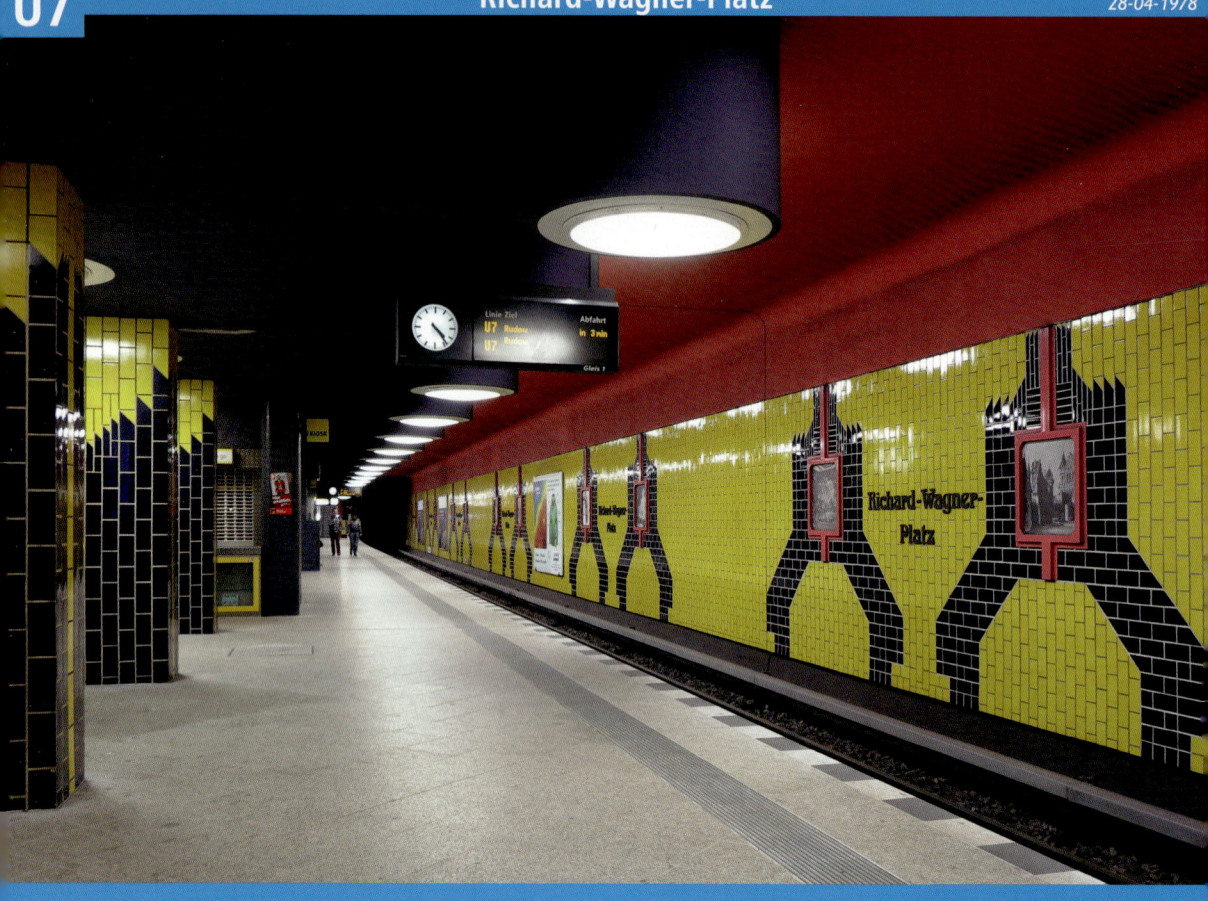

Im U-Bhf **Richard-Wagner-Platz**, der den früheren Kleinprofilbahnhof der ehemaligen Linie 5 ersetzte, zieren Szenen aus Wagners Opern die roten Schaukästen an den Wänden. 2013 wurde der Boden mit Granitplatten belegt, was dem Bahnhof zusammen mit der vor einigen Jahren verbesserten Beleuchtung ein freundlicheres Aussehen verleiht. Am nordöstlichen Zugang (rechts) wurde ein Portal des alten Bahnhofs wiederverwendet.

Am U-Bhf **Bismarckstraße**, der im Vergleich zu den Fliesenmustern der benachbarten Stationen eher nüchtern wirkt, kann man über etwas verschachtelt angeordnete Roll- und Festtreppen zur U2 umsteigen, die auf der oberen Ebene hält. Ein Umbau steht daher an.

Der U-Bhf **Wilmersdorfer Straße** unter der gleichnamigen Fußgängerzone wurde 2007 modernisiert, indem die einst dunklen Säulen nun hellbeige verkleidet wurden und auch hier ein Granitboden verlegt wurde. Das Fliesenmotiv an den Wänden stellt eine stilisierte Lilie dar, eine Blume, die im Bezirkswappen von Wilmersdorf zu sehen ist. Der S-Bhf Charlottenburg rückte 2006 näher an die U-Bahn heran.

Richard-Wagner-Platz station, which replaced the old small-profile station on the former line 5, is decorated with scenes from Wagner's operas displayed in red cases along the walls. In 2013, the floor was covered with granite slabs, which, together with the improved lighting introduced a few years ago, gives the station a much more pleasant appearance. At the northeastern entrance (right), a portal of the old station was reused.

Compared to the tile patterns found in the neighbouring stations, Bismarckstraße looks rather sober. Interchange with line U2 on the upper level is provided via stairs and escalators arranged in a somewhat user-unfriendly way, which is why the rebuilding of the station is planned.

Wilmersdorfer Straße station lies below a pedestrian zone and was modernised in 2007, when the previously dark columns were reclad with beige panels and a granite floor was laid. The tile pattern on the walls depicts a stylised lily, a flower found in the coat of arms of the district of Wilmersdorf. In 2006, the S-Bahn station Charlottenburg was moved closer to the U-Bahn.

28-04-1978 **Bismarckstraße** **U7**

28-04-1978 **Wilmersdorfer Straße** **U7**

107

U7 — Adenauerplatz — 28-04-1978

Der U-Bhf **Adenauerplatz** liegt quer unter dem Kurfürstendamm, darunter befindet sich der komplette Rohbau eines Bahnhofs für die seit 1913 an der Uhlandstraße endende Linie (heute U1). Der U7-Bahnhof wurde 2005 modernisiert, indem die Wände neu gestrichen wurden, wobei das ursprüngliche stilisierte A nun in geänderter Form erscheint. Außerdem wurden die vertikalen Flächen auf dem Bahnsteig mit weißen Emailplatten verkleidet und ein Granitboden verlegt.

Vergleichsweise original präsentiert sich der U-Bhf **Konstanzer Straße**, auch wenn die einst orangefarbenen Stationsschilder von Standardschildern verdrängt wurden. Im Mai 2008 wurde ein auf dem Mittelstreifen der Brandenburgischen Straße mündender nördlicher Ausgang (rechts) eröffnet.

Der U-Bhf **Fehrbelliner Platz** wurde bereits Ende der 1990er Jahre modernisiert, wobei jedoch die typischen abgerundeten Elemente der 1970er Jahre erhalten blieben. An der Oberfläche befindet sich eines der markantesten Eingangsgebäude der Berliner U-Bahn, auch ein Werk von Rainer G. Rümmler (siehe S. 97).

Adenauerplatz station lies under the road intersection with Kurfürstendamm, and also features a complete unused station shell for the line that since 1913 has terminated at Uhlandstraße (now U1). The U7 station was modernised in 2005, with the walls being repainted, although with the original stylised A now appearing in a different form. In addition, the vertical surfaces on the platform were clad with white enamelled panels and a granite floor was laid.

Konstanzer Straße station has been largely preserved in its original style, even though the old orange station signs have been replaced with standard signs. In May 2008, a new exit located in the median strip of Brandenburgische Straße was opened at the northern end of the station (above).

Fehrbelliner Platz station was already modernised in the late 1990s, but its rounded elements, typical of the 1970s, were preserved. On the surface, one of the most iconic entrance buildings on the Berlin U-Bahn can be seen, another work by Rainer G. Rümmler (see page 97).

28-04-1978 **Konstanzer Straße** **U7**

29-01-1971 **Fehrbelliner Platz** **U7**

U7 — Blissestraße — 29-01-1971

Im gekrümmten U-Bhf **Blissestraße** richtet sich das Hauptaugenmerk der Gestaltung nicht wie sonst meist auf die Hintergleiswände, sondern auf die Decke. Diese besteht aus unzähligen, verschieden tiefen Gipskassetten, die schalldämpfend wirken sollen.

Am U-Bhf **Berliner Straße** kann man zur auf der oberen Ebene kreuzenden U9 umsteigen. Beide Bahnsteigebenen wurden 2000/2001 modernisiert und bekamen weiße Wandfliesen und einen Granitboden. Anders als bei der U9 waren die Hintergleiswände auf der U7-Ebene von Anfang an mit roten Emailblechen verkleidet. Die Farbkombination Rot/Weiß soll auf die Berliner Stadtfarben anspielen.

Die Landesfarben Bayerns folgen dementsprechend im benachbarten U-Bhf **Bayerischer Platz**, der zudem im Bayerischen Viertel liegt. Außerdem ist hier die auf beiden Bahnsteigseiten entgegengesetzte Deckenstruktur erwähnenswert, die das Licht jeweils nur in Fahrtrichtung fallen lässt. An der Südseite der Grunewaldstraße befindet sich ein farblich dazu abgestimmtes Eingangsgebäude, das im Zuge des Baus der U7 errichtet wurde (unten).

Berliner Straß

Blissestraße station lies in a curve. While the main focus of the design in other stations is on the walls behind the tracks, here it is on the ceiling, which consists of numerous plaster boxes of various depths that are supposed to be sound-absorbent.

At *Berliner Straße*, transfer to line U9 is available on the upper level. Both platform levels were modernised in 2000/2001, when they received white wall tiles and a granite floor. Unlike line U9, the side walls on the U7 level had been covered with red enamelled panels right from the beginning. The colour scheme of red and white may have been inspired by Berlin's city colours.

Accordingly, the national colours of Bavaria follow in the next station *Bayerischer Platz*, which furthermore lies in a neighbourhood known as Bayerisches Viertel. Noteworthy here is the ceiling, whose inclination on either side of the platform is opposite, with lights shining only in the direction of travel. The entrance building on the south side of Grunewaldstraße, also white and blue, was built together with line U7 (left).

Berliner Straße — U7
29-01-1971

▶ U9

Bayerischer Platz — U7
29-01-1971

▶ U4

U7 — Eisenacher Straße — 29-01-1971

Vielleicht inspiriert durch den Thüringer Wald, an dessen Nordrand die Stadt Eisenach liegt, wurde der U-Bhf **Eisenacher Straße** mit grünen Eternitplatten an den Wänden verkleidet, während die Mittelstützen gelb gefliest sind. Auffällig ist die gewölbte, indirekt beleuchtete Decke.

Der U-Bhf **Kleistpark** war als Umsteigestation zur „U10" konzipiert, für die unter dem U7-Bahnsteig ein 40 m langer Rohbau mitgebaut wurde. Gestalterisch liegt dieser Bahnhof zwischen den typischen, in den 1960er Jahren entstandenen Stationen auf dem Abschnitt bis Britz-Süd mit ihren kleinteiligen Wandverfliesungen und dem abwechslungsreicheren Stil der 1970er. An den Wänden wurden hier großflächige Fliesen angebracht, die Stützen hingegen mit Aluminiumblechen verkleidet.

Der U-Bhf **Yorckstraße** liegt zwischen den beiden Stationen der Nord-Süd-S-Bahn, die man jeweils über einen kurzen Weg auf dem Bürgersteig erreicht. Der 11 m breite Bahnsteig wird durch eine doppelte Stützenreihe gegliedert, die im Stil der Zeit mit weißen horizontalen Riemchen verkleidet ist, die Wände kontrastieren dazu in Orange.

Perhaps inspired by the Thuringian Forest, at the northern edge of which the town of Eisenach is located, *Eisenacher Straße* station is clad with green asbestos cement panels on the walls, with the central columns tiled in yellow. A more distinctive feature is the vaulted, indirectly illuminated ceiling.

Kleistpark station was conceived as an interchange with line 'U10', for which a 40 m long section was built under the U7 platform. In terms of design, it can be placed between the typical stations on the section to Britz-Süd built in the 1960s with their small-tile wall coverings, and the more varied styles of the 1970s. Here the walls have large tiles, while the central pillars are clad with aluminium sheets.

Yorckstraße station is located between the two S-Bahn stations on the north-south route, each of which can be reached via a short walk on the surface. The 11 m wide platform is divided by a double row of columns, which are clad with white horizontally-placed rectangular tiles, the typical style at the time, with the walls contrasting in orange.

Kleistpark — U7

Yorckstraße — U7

U7 — Möckernbrücke — 28-02-1966

▶ U1

Gestalterisch passt der U-Bhf **Möckernbrücke** zu den wenige Jahre zuvor eröffneten Bahnhöfen Richtung Britz-Süd, mit ockergelben Riemchen an den Hintergleiswänden und blauen im Bahnsteigbereich, eine ähnliche Kombination wie im U-Bhf Güntzelstraße auf der U9. Der U7-Bahnhof liegt südlich des Landwehrkanals, zum Hochbahnhof der U1 gelangt man über eine eingehauste Brücke (rechts).

Der U-Bhf **Mehringdamm** entstand schon wie die nun folgenden Stationen in den 1920er Jahren als Teil der „Nordsüdbahn" (später Linie C, heute U6). Er wurde in den 1960er Jahren für die U7 von einem dreigleisigen Verzweigungsbahnhof in einen viergleisigen Kreuzungsbahnhof mit Umsteigen auf demselben Bahnsteig umgebaut. Das ursprüngliche Deckengewölbe wurde erst 2012 im Zuge einer Grundsanierung wieder freigelegt (siehe U6).

Die Deckenstruktur und Eisenstützen sowie die Lage direkt unter der Oberfläche lassen erkennen, dass der U-Bhf **Gneisenaustraße** zur „Nordsüdbahn" gehörte. Für die U7 wurde der Bahnsteig in den 1960er Jahren verlängert und die Wände grün gefliest.

Möckernbrüc

Möckernbrücke station is similar to those opened on the section to Britz-Süd a few years earlier. The walls have small rectangular tiles in ochre, while the vertical surfaces on the platform are blue, a colour combination similar to that found at Güntzelstraße on line U9. The U7 station is located south of the Landwehrkanal and is connected to the elevated U1 station via an encased bridge (above).

Like the following stations, **Mehringdamm** was already built in the 1920s as part of the 'Nordsüdbahn' (later line C, now U6). For line U7, it was rebuilt in the 1960s from a three-track junction into a four-track cross-platform interchange. The original vaults were only uncovered in 2012, when the entire station was renovated (see U6).

The ceiling structure and iron supports, as well as its location just below the surface, reveal that **Gneisenaustraße** station also once belonged to the 'Nordsüdbahn'. When the platform was extended for line U7 in the 1960s, the previously uncovered walls were tiled in green.

19-04-1924 **Mehringdamm** **U7**

▶ U6

19-04-1924 **Gneisenaustraße** **U7**

U7 — Südstern — 14-12-1924

Der U-Bhf **Südstern** war 1924 der erste Bahnhof der „Nordsüdbahn", dessen Wände nicht nur gestrichen, sondern mit glasierten Zementplatten verkleidet wurden. Die Ausgänge lagen ursprünglich an den Bahnsteigenden, wurden aber 1958 im Zuge der Bahnsteigverlängerung in die Mitte verlegt, von wo sie in einen Pavillon münden. Am östlichen Ende des Bahnhofs wurde 2009 ein Aufzug eingebaut.

Der U-Bhf **Hermannplatz** gehört wegen seiner imposanten U7-Bahnsteighalle zu den bekanntesten der Berliner U-Bahn. Der riesige Raum mit den 7 m hohen Säulen wird mittig durch die eine Ebene höher kreuzende U8 geteilt. Beide Ebenen entstanden gleichzeitig und sind demnach sehr ähnlich gestaltet. Die gesamte Anlage wurde 1990/91 weitgehend originalgetreu neu verfliest. In Bahnsteigmitte führt ein Aufgang direkt ins Kaufhaus Karstadt. Wie bei den folgenden Stationen im Zentrum von Neukölln ist der Ursprung dieses Abschnitts noch an den typischen gezackten „Nordsüd"-Portalen zu erkennen.

In 1924, **Südstern** became the first station on the 'Nordsüdbahn' to have its walls not just painted, but clad with glazed cement slabs. Originally, the exits were at the ends of the platform, but in 1958, when the platform was extended, they were moved to the centre to lead into a surface pavilion. A lift was installed at the eastern end of the station in 2009.

Because of its impressive U7 station hall, **Hermannplatz** is one of the best-known stations on the Berlin U-Bahn system. The huge space with its 7 m high columns is divided in the middle by the trough that carries line U8 across on the upper level. The two station levels were built at the same time and therefore have a similar design. The entire station complex was retiled in 1990/91 using ceramic tiles almost identical to the originals. In the middle of the platform, an exit leads directly into the Karstadt department store. Like at the following stations in the centre of Neukölln, the typical jagged 'Nordsüd' portals indicate the origin of this section.

Hermannplatz U7

1-04-1926

U7 — Rathaus Neukölln

11-04-1926

Gestalterisch bilden die U-Bahnhöfe **Rathaus Neukölln** (blau) und **Karl-Marx-Straße** (grün) eine Einheit, wobei eine sehr ähnliche Wandverkleidung auch am Südstern zu finden ist. Hier wurden erstmals auf der „Nordsüdbahn" die Mittelstützen mit Kacheln verkleidet. Beide Stationen liegen in einfacher Tiefenlage. Am U-Bhf Rathaus Neukölln wurde nachträglich in Bahnsteigmitte eine Fahrtreppe eingebaut, die wie die Ausgänge in die Fahrbahnmitte der Karl-Marx-Straße mündet. Der U-Bhf Karl-Marx-Straße wurde bereits Anfang der 1990er Jahre saniert, der U-Bhf Rathaus Neukölln folgte einige Jahre später, wobei hier ein Aufzug hinzukam und auch der Asphaltboden verschwand.

Am U-Bhf **Neukölln** (Südring) besteht eine Umsteigemöglichkeit zur Ringbahn, die nach der Stilllegung von 1980 seit 1993 wieder hier hält. Ein direkter Aufzug verbindet beide Bahnsteige. Die zitronengelbe Station ist gestalterisch eine Mischung der Standardtypen der „Nordsüdbahn" (U6), der „GN-Bahn" (U8) und der „Friedrichsfelder Linie" (U5), die alle Ende der 1920er Jahre entstanden. Sie wurde Ende der 1990er Jahre saniert. Dabei wurden bräunliche Bodenplatten verlegt.

Neukölln

The underground stations **Rathaus Neukölln** (blue) and **Karl-Marx-Straße** (green) are almost identical, with a wall cladding very similar to that at Südstern. For the first time on the 'Nordsüdbahn', the centre supports were covered with tiles, too. Both stations are located just below street level. At Rathaus Neukölln, an escalator was later added in the middle of the platform, which, like the exits, surfaces on the median of Karl-Marx-Straße. Karl-Marx-Straße station was modernised in the early 1990s, followed by Rathaus Neukölln some years later, here with a lift and a new floor with stone slabs.

At **Neukölln** (Südring), passengers can change to the circular S-Bahn route, which, having closed in 1980, has been operating again since 1993. A single lift connects the two platforms. The lemon-yellow station is a mix of the standard designs developed for the 'Nordsüdbahn' (U6), the 'GN-Bahn' (U8) and the 'Friedrichsfelder Linie' (U5), which were all built in the late 1920s. It was renovated in the late 1990s, when brownish floor slabs were laid.

Karl-Marx-Straße — U7
11-04-1926

Neukölln — U7
1-12-1930

U7 — Grenzallee — 21-12-1930

Der U-Bhf **Grenzallee** war 33 Jahre lang Endstation des Neuköllner Astes der Linie C. Gestalterisch ähnelt er dem Nachbarbahnhof Neukölln, hier mit der Kennfarbe Hellgrün. Ende der 1990er Jahre wurden graue Bodenplatten verlegt und auch hier die Beleuchtung verbessert.

Mit 1241 m Abstand liegt der U-Bhf **Blaschkoallee** relativ weit von Grenzallee entfernt. Da die U7 ursprünglich im offenen Trog gebaut werden sollte, liegen alle Stationen bis Zwickauer Damm in einfacher Tiefenlage, wodurch statt eines Zwischengeschosses mehr oder weniger spektakuläre Eingangsgebäude (unten) entstanden. Der U-Bhf Blaschkoallee wird derzeit generalsaniert und erhält einen Aufzug. Bis 2012 waren die Wände mit weißen horizontalen Riemchen verkleidet, die Stützen hingegen hatten eine Ziegelverblendung. In den frühen 1960er Jahren kam statt des später wieder eingeführten Asphaltbodens ein Bodenbelag aus Kunststeinplatten zur Anwendung.

Sehr ähnlich sieht es im U-Bhf **Parchimer Allee** aus, nur dass hier die Wände blau und die Stützen weiß verkleidet sind. Die ursprünglichen Holzbänke wurden auch hier durch Drahtgitterstühle ersetzt.

Parchimer Allee

For 33 years, **Grenzallee** station was the terminus of line C's Neukölln branch. Its design resembles the neighbouring Neukölln station, although here in a bright green tone. In the late 1990s, grey floor tiles were laid and the lighting was improved.

At 1241 m, **Blaschkoallee** station is rather far from Grenzallee. Since line U7 was initially meant to be built in an open cutting, all the stations from here to Zwickauer Damm lie just below the surface, with rather functional entrance buildings (left) instead of mezzanines. This station is currently being renovated and a lift is being installed. Until 2012, the walls were covered with small white horizontal tiles while the supports had a red brick veneer. In the early 1960s, instead of the standard asphalt floor, which came back later, the platform floor here was covered with artificial stone slabs.

Parchimer Allee looks very similar, except that the walls are blue and the columns white. The original wooden benches were also replaced here with wire mesh chairs.

Blaschkoallee

Blaschkoallee
28-09-1963 — U7

Parchimer Allee
28-09-1963 — U7

U7 — Britz-Süd — 28-09-1963

Bei seiner Inbetriebnahme 1963 war der U-Bhf **Britz-Süd** noch Endpunkt der Linie C, bis dann 1966 die eigenständige Linie 7 geschaffen wurde. Da es hier ursprünglich nur einen Zugang am südlichen Bahnsteigende gab, wurde im Zuge eines netzweiten Nachrüstprogramms zur Verbesserung der Fluchtwege im Fall von Bränden 2003 ein Nordzugang eröffnet. Zur Verschönerung der braunen Hintergleiswände wurden 2011 weiße Fliesenflächen mit Motiven aus dem nahen Britzer Garten angebracht. Gleichzeitig wurde ein hellerer Bodenbelag verlegt.

Der südliche Eingang am U-Bhf **Johannisthaler Chaussee** (Gropiusstadt) wurde Ende der 1990er Jahre in den Eingangsbereich des Einkaufszentrums „Gropius-Passagen" integriert. Gleichzeitig wurde der nördliche Eingang (rechts) umgebaut und die gesamte Station modernisiert, wobei die Mittelstützen eine Edelstahlverkleidung bekamen.

Waren weiter nördlich noch Spaltriemchen typisch, so sind auf dem nächsten Abschnitt wie im U-Bhf **Lipschitzallee** Großkeramikplatten als Wandverkleidung (hier weiß/dunkelgrau) charakteristisch.

Opened in 1963, **Britz-Süd** was the terminus of line C, until the independent line 7 was established in 1966. Since originally there was only one access at the southern end of the platform, a northern entrance was opened in 2003 as part of a network-wide upgrade programme to improve the emergency exits for fire safety reasons. To embellish the brown walls, white tiled surfaces with motifs inspired by the nearby Britzer Garten were added in 2011. At the same time, a brighter floor was laid.

In the late 1990s, the southern entrance at **Johannisthaler Chaussee** (Gropiusstadt) station was integrated into the lobby of the 'Gropius-Passagen' shopping centre. At the same time, the northern entrance (above) was rebuilt and the entire station modernised, with the supports being clad with stainless steel sheets.

While on the section further north, small rectangular tiles are typical, on the next section the stations feature large ceramic plates on the walls — here at **Lipschitzallee** in a white and dark grey colour scheme.

Johannisthaler Chaussee — U7

02-01-1970

Lipschitzallee — U7

02-01-1970

U7 — Wutzkyallee

02-01-1970

Der U-Bhf **Wutzkyallee** erhielt ein zum benachbarten Bahnhof Lipschitzallee umgekehrtes Farbschema, auch wenn statt des Dunkelgrau ein graublauer Farbton verwendet wurde. In beiden Stationen liegen die Aufgänge mittig unter einem Eingangspavillon. Dieser wurde im Fall von Wutzkyallee im Jahr 2012 umgebaut (rechts) und direkt an ein neues kleines Einkaufszentrum angeschlossen.

Ein Eingangsgebäude mit einem markanten Dach unterscheidet den U-Bahnhof **Zwickauer Damm**. Die Treppenwände sind mit Ziegeln verblendet, während die Stützen bis 2012 mit schwarzen Kacheln verkleidet waren.

Mit einer Wandverkleidung aus Asbestzementplatten, hier in Orangerot, ähnelt der Endbahnhof **Rudow** den U7-Stationen Bayerischer Platz und Eisenacher Straße, die etwa zeitgleich entstanden. Die Mittelstützen erhielten eine Aluminiumverkleidung. Da sich der einzige Ausgang am südlichen Bahnsteigende befand, wurde 2008 am nördlichen Ende ein zweiter eröffnet. Ein Aufzug war mittig bereits 1993 eingebaut worden.

Wutzkyallee

The colour scheme at **Wutzkyallee** station is the inverse of that found at the neighbouring Lipschitzallee station, although instead of the dark grey, a grey-blue tone was used. In both stations, the staircases are in the middle of the platform and lead to an entrance pavilion. The one at Wutzkyallee was rebuilt in 2012 (above) and connected directly to a new small shopping centre.

An entrance building with a peculiar roof distinguishes **Zwickauer Damm** station. While the walls bordering the stairs are veneered with bricks, the columns used to be covered with black tiles until 2012.

With a wall cladding of asbestos cement panels, here in orange, the terminus **Rudow** is similar to the U7 stations Bayerischer Platz and Eisenacher Straße, which were built around the same time. The centre supports are hidden behind aluminium sheets. Originally the only exit was at the southern end of the platform, but in 2008 a second exit was opened at the northern end. A lift had already been installed in the middle of the station in 1993.

02-01-1970 — **Zwickauer Damm** — **U7**

01-07-1972 — **Rudow** — **U7**

U8 Wittenau – Hermannstraße

Rosenthaler Platz

Die heutige Linie U8 entstand in den 1920er Jahren als *GN-Bahn* (Gesundbrunnen – Neukölln), nachdem Pläne für eine Schwebebahn nach Wuppertaler Vorbild ad acta gelegt worden waren. Der Bau hatte unter der Regie der AEG bereits vor dem Ersten Weltkrieg begonnen (einzelne Stationen in damals üblicher einfacher Tiefenlage sind Zeugnis davon), doch schließlich wurde die nun als Linie D bezeichnete Strecke von der Stadt Berlin in den 1920er Jahren, den Boom-Jahren des Berliner U-Bahn-Baus, vollendet.

Wie bei der U6 verwandelten sich zahlreiche Bahnhöfe der U8 auf dem zentralen Abschnitt mit dem Bau der Berliner Mauer 1961 in Geisterbahnhöfe, die die Züge der West-Berliner BVG ohne Halt durchfahren mussten, auf dem Nordabschnitt blieben bis 1977 lediglich zwei Stationen auf West-Berliner Gebiet.

Today's line U8 was opened in the 1920s as the 'GN-Bahn' (for Gesundbrunnen — Neukölln), after plans for a suspended railway of the Wuppertal type had been shelved. Construction had already started under the direction of the AEG [Allgemeine Elektricitäts-Gesellschaft] before World War I (some stations were then still built just below street level, as was typical at the time), but eventually, what became known as line D was completed by the City of Berlin in the 1920s, the boom years of Berlin U-Bahn construction.

As with line U6, numerous U8 stations on the central portion became ghost stations when the Berlin Wall was erected in 1961. West Berlin BVG trains had to skip these stations, and until 1977, they only served two stations in West Berlin territory on the line's northern section.

Paracelsus-Bad

U8

18.2 km (gänzlich unterirdisch | *completely underground*)
24 Bahnhöfe | *stations*

17-07-1927: Schönleinstraße – Boddinstraße
12-02-1928: Schönleinstraße – Kottbusser Tor
06-04-1928: Kottbusser Tor – Heinrich-Heine-Straße
04-08-1929: Boddinstraße – Leinestraße
18-04-1930: Heinrich-Heine-Straße – Gesundbrunnen
13-08-1961: [X] Bernauer Straße, Rosenthaler Platz, Weinmeisterstraße, Alexanderplatz, Jannowitzbrücke, Heinrich-Heine-Straße
05-10-1977: Gesundbrunnen – Osloer Straße
27-04-1987: Osloer Straße – Paracelsus-Bad
11-11-1989: +* Jannowitzbrücke
22-12-1989: +* Rosenthaler Platz
12-04-1990: +* Bernauer Straße
01-07-1990: +* Weinmeisterstraße, Alexanderplatz, Heinrich-Heine-Straße
24-09-1994: Paracelsus-Bad – Wittenau
13-07-1996: Leinestraße – Hermannstraße

[X] Schließung | *Closure*   * Wiederinbetriebnahme | *Reopening*

Wittenau

Bereits vor dem Fall der Mauer war damit begonnen worden, die U8 Richtung Reinickendorf zu verlängern, mit dem Ziel, die Stadtrandsiedlung Märkisches Viertel anzuschließen. Mit der Wiedervereinigung der Stadt wurden neue Prioritäten festgelegt, so dass die U8 zwar 1994 den S-Bahnhof Wittenau erreichte, das kurze Stück bis zum Märkischen Viertel aber bis heute nicht verwirklicht worden ist.

Am südlichen Ende fand 1996 ein Lückenschluss statt, so dass man am Bahnhof Hermannstraße nun bequem zur seit 1993 wieder befahrenen Ringbahn umsteigen kann. Eine weitere Verlängerung Richtung Süden ist nicht vorgesehen.

Während die älteren Stationen fast durchweg aus der Hand von Alfred Grenander stammen, sorgte auf dem Nordabschnitt Rainer G. Rümmler für Abwechslung.

Even before the collapse of the Wall, the construction of an extension towards the district of Reinickendorf had eventually started to serve the large housing estate called Märkisches Viertel. The reunification of the city brought with it new priorities, and although line U8 reached S-Bahn station Wittenau in 1994, the short, remaining section to Märkisches Viertel never materialised.

At the southern end, the short gap between Leinestraße and Hermannstraße was closed in 1996 to allow interchange between line U8 and the S-Bahn ring line, which had reopened in 1993. An extension further south is not planned.

While most of the older stations were designed by Alfred Grenander, Rainer G. Rümmler provided an interesting variety of architecture on the northern extension.

Lindauer Allee

Erfahren Sie mehr über diese Linie in unserer Reihe:

Berliner U-Bahn-Linien: U8 – Die „GN-Bahn" von Gesundbrunnen nach Neukölln

von Alexander Seefeldt

Planung · Bau
Betrieb · Stationen

ISBN 978-3-936573-40-4
(erscheint voraussl. 2014)

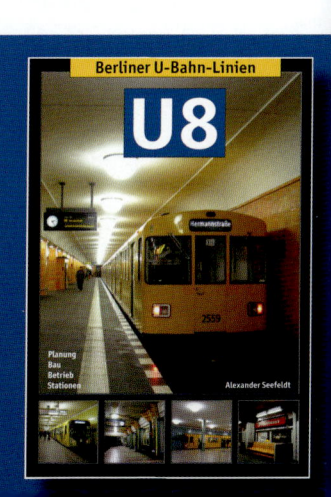

U8 — Wittenau — 24-09-1994

Die drei nördlichsten Stationen der U8 sind geprägt von mächtigen Säulen. Im Endbahnhof **Wittenau** (Wilhelmsruher Damm) sind diese mit grünen und gelben Fliesen verkleidet, gelbe Verkleidungselemente gliedern die Decke. Neuartig war in den 1980er Jahren auch die auf die restliche Bahnhofsgestaltung abgestimmte Anordnung und Farbe der Bodenplatten. Vom östlichen Zwischengeschoss besteht ein direkter Übergang zur S-Bahn, deren Bahnsteig bei dieser Gelegenheit nach Süden verlängert wurde.

Die roten Backsteine im U-Bhf **Rathaus Reinickendorf** setzen den Stil des namensgebenden Gebäudes fort. Das südliche Eingangsgebäude (rechts) liegt über einem Kanal, dem Nordgraben.

Ebenfalls vom namensgebenden Gebäude inspiriert wurde der U-Bhf **Karl-Bonhoeffer-Nervenklinik**. Wie beim vorigen Bahnhof schränkt die doppelte Reihe der wuchtigen Pfeiler die Übersichtlichkeit des Bahnsteigbereichs stark ein. Die Kombination aus roten und gelben Backsteinen findet man häufig auch bei der Berliner S-Bahn, deren gleichnamige Station hier allerdings ca. 300 m entfernt liegt.

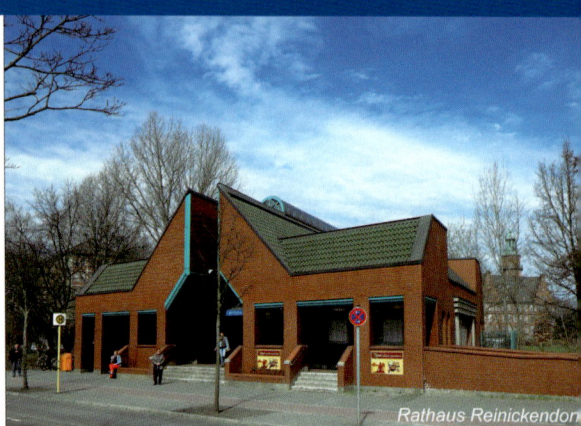

Rathaus Reinickendorf

The northernmost three U8 stations are dominated by massive columns. At the terminus **Wittenau** (Wilhelmsruher Damm), they are clad in green and yellow tiles, while yellow trim elements give structure to the ceiling. A novelty of the 1980s, the configuration and colour of the floor plates match the rest of the station design. Interchange with the S-Bahn is available from the eastern mezzanine, with the S-Bahn platform having been extended south when the U-Bahn opened.

The red brick design at **Rathaus Reinickendorf** station is an extension of the architectural style found at the town hall the station is named after. The southern entrance building (above) was built over the Nordgraben canal.

Karl-Bonhoeffer-Nervenklinik station was also inspired by its namesake. Like at the previous station, the double row of massive pillars greatly restricts the view through the platform area. The combination of red and yellow bricks is often found on the Berlin S-Bahn, whose station of the same name, however, lies about 300 m away.

Karl-Bonhoeffer-Nervenklinik

Rathaus Reinickendorf — U8
24-09-1994

Karl-Bonhoeffer-Nervenklinik — U8
24-09-1994

U8 — Lindauer Allee — 24-09-1994

Wie im Wappen der Stadt Lindau am Bodensee ist die Linde, wenn auch in stark stilisierter Form (rechts), das Leitmotiv im U-Bhf **Lindauer Allee**, dem einzigen der U8 mit Seitenbahnsteigen und mit einer sehr charakteristischen Balustrade. Der leicht türkisfarbene Grundton der Station findet sich selbst in den Bodenplatten wieder.

7½ Jahre lang war **Paracelsus-Bad** nördlicher Endpunkt der U8. Der durch die schwarz-weiße Gestaltung etwas klinisch wirkende U-Bahnhof ist ganz dem Thema Wellness und Heilkunde gewidmet, die Wände sind mit Badeszenen aus dem Mittelalter verziert (siehe Seite 126). Dieser U-Bahnhof war von Anfang an mit einem Aufzug ausgestattet.

Nach einem scharfen Knick erreicht die U8 den U-Bhf **Residenzstraße**, dessen Gestaltung durch den Regierungssitz der preußischen Könige beeinflusst wurde. An den Wänden sind deshalb Ansichten des (bald wieder aufzubauenden) Berliner Stadtschlosses (unten) sowie historische Pläne der Stadt zu sehen.

At **Lindauer Allee** station, just like in the coat-of-arms of the town of Lindau on Lake Constance, the main theme is the lime tree, although in a highly stylised form (above). This is the only station on line U8 with side platforms and a very iconic balustrade. The station's light turquoise colour scheme is even found on the floor slabs.

For 7 ½ years, **Paracelsus-Bad** was the northern terminus of line U8. The black and white design creates a rather sanitary ambience, ideal for the wellness and health theme chosen here: the walls depict bath scenes from the Middle Ages (see p. 126). A lift has been available in this station from the very beginning.

After a sharp bend, line U8 reaches **Residenzstraße** station, whose design was influenced by the fact that Berlin was the government seat of the Prussian kings. Views of the (soon to be rebuilt) 'Berliner Stadtschloss' [Berlin Royal Palace] (left) as well as historical maps of the city can therefore be seen on the walls.

Residenzstraße

27-04-1987 — **Paracelsus-Bad** — **U8**

27-04-1987 — **Residenzstraße** — **U8**

U8 — Franz-Neumann-Platz — 27-04-1987

Der U-Bhf **Franz-Neumann-Platz** trägt nicht nur an den Stationswänden, sondern sogar auf den meisten Netzplänen den Zusatz **Am Schäfersee**. Die Parklandschaft um diesen nahegelegenen See inspirierte wohl auch Architekt Rainer G. Rümmler dazu, die mächtigen Säulen in stilisierte Bäume zu verwandeln. Das Baummotiv wiederholt sich an den Seitenwänden.

Bereits in den 1970er Jahren versuchte man, die Gestaltung der U-Bahnhöfe in Verbindung mit deren Namen bzw. Umgebung zu bringen. So zieren norwegische Flaggen die Wände im U-Bhf **Osloer Straße**, der ansonsten 2004 umgestaltet wurde. Statt der früheren Aluminium-Wandverkleidung hängen nun dunkelblaue Emailplatten und ein freundlicher Granitboden löste den früher typischen Asphaltboden ab.

Der Schriftzug an den Seitenwänden verrät ganz eindeutig, dass der U-Bhf **Pankstraße** in den 1970er Jahren gebaut wurde. Andere Elemente aus jener Epoche sind leider im Laufe der Zeit verschwunden, demnächst soll die Vorhalle des U-Bahnhofs modernisiert werden.

Franz-Neumann-Platz station carries the name tag '**Am Schäfersee**' not only on the station walls, but also on most network maps. The park around this nearby lake probably inspired architect Rainer G. Rümmler when he transformed the massive columns into stylised trees. The tree motif is repeated on the walls.

Already by the 1970s, Berlin's U-Bahn architects had begun relating a station's design to its name or surroundings. The Norwegian flag therefore still adorns the walls of **Osloer Straße** station, while the rest of it was restyled in 2004, when the original aluminium panelling was replaced by dark blue enamelled plates, and the typical asphalt by a friendly granite floor.

The font type chosen for the station name on the walls reveals quite clearly that **Pankstraße** station was built in the 1970s. Other elements from that period have unfortunately disappeared over the years. The station mezzanine is soon to be modernised.

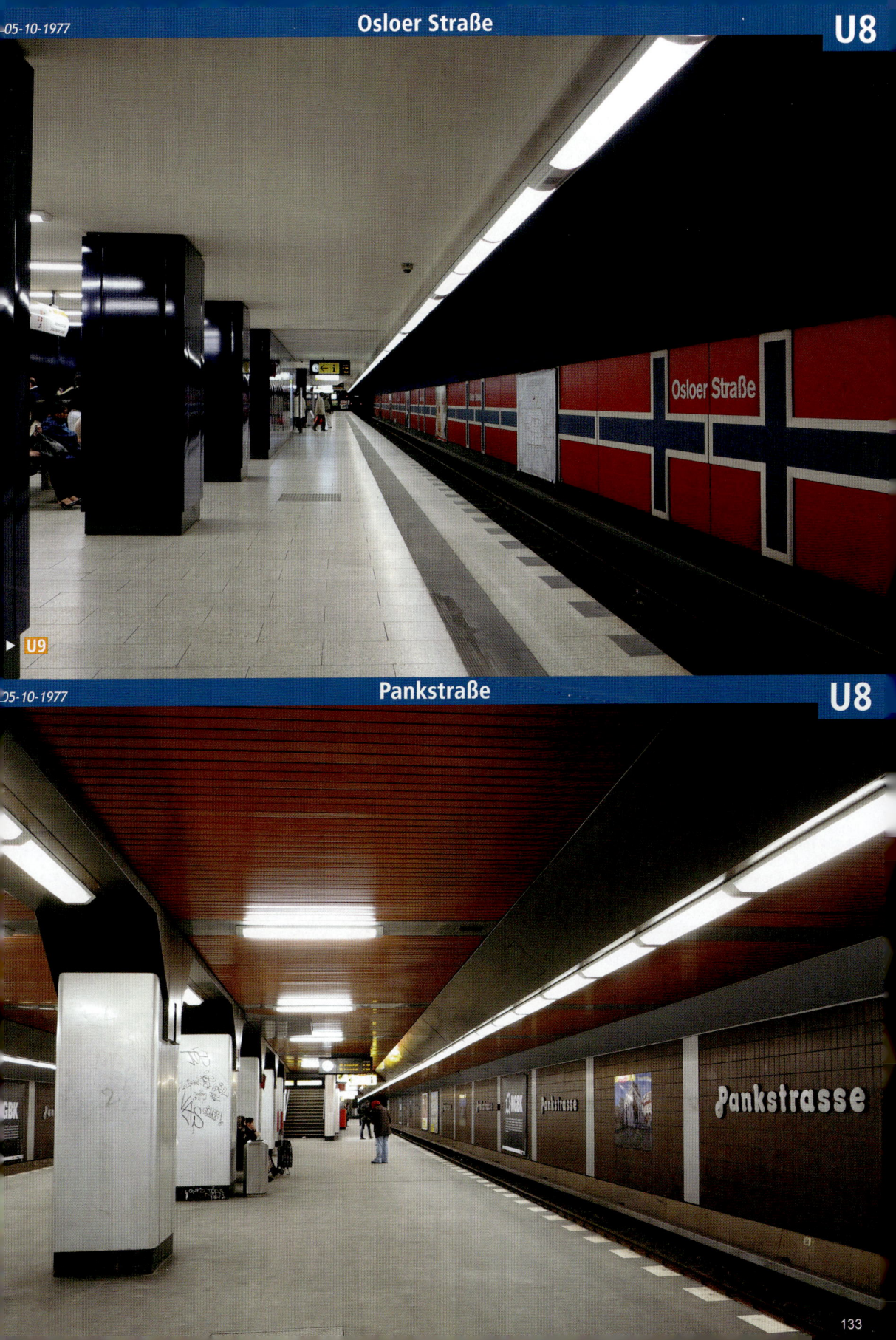

| Osloer Straße | U8 |

05-10-1977

U9

| Pankstraße | U8 |

05-10-1977

U8 Gesundbrunnen 18-04-1930

Der U-Bhf **Gesundbrunnen** wurde relativ tief angelegt, da die Trasse hier die im Einschnitt verlaufende Ringbahn unterquert. Der Bahnsteigbereich wurde Anfang des Jahrtausends grundsaniert. Am nördlichen Bahnhofsende befindet sich ein freistehendes Eingangsgebäude, eher eine Seltenheit für diese Epoche. Der südliche Eingang war bis vor Kurzem in eine Häuserzeile integriert (unten). Feste Treppen führen seit 2001 direkt zu den beiden Bahnsteigen der S-Bahn.

Der Bau der U-Bahnhöfe **Voltastraße** und **Bernauer Straße** begann bereits vor dem Ersten Weltkrieg, weshalb beide nach damaligem Standard ohne Zwischengeschosse in einfacher Tiefenlage ausgeführt wurden. In beiden Stationen fallen die auf dieser Linie nur hier zu findenden eleganten Steinsäulen auf. Die Wandverfliesung im U-Bhf Voltastraße wurde bereits 2011 erneuert, die Decke ist noch in Arbeit. Der U-Bhf Bernauer Straße wurde schon in den 1990er Jahren renoviert. Letzterer lag direkt südlich der Berliner Mauer und blieb deshalb wie die folgenden Stationen von 1961 bis 1990 geschlossen.

The underground station at **Gesundbrunnen** lies rather deep because the line had to cross the S-Bahn's ring corridor, which runs in a trench at this point. The platform area was renovated at the beginning of the millennium. At the northern end, the station features a freestanding entrance building, a rarity for this period. Until recently, the southern entrance was integrated into a row of houses (left). Since 2001, two direct sets of stairs have connected the U-Bahn station with the two S-Bahn platforms.

The construction of the underground stations at **Voltastraße** and **Bernauer Straße** began before the First World War, and as was the standard at the time, they were built just below street level and without mezzanines. They are the only two stations on line U8 that have elegant stone columns. While the wall tiles at Voltastraße were already replaced in 2011, the ceiling is still under refurbishment. Bernauer Straße had been renovated in the 1990s. The latter was located directly south of the Berlin Wall, and therefore like the following stations, it remained closed from 1961 until 1990.

18-04-1930 — **Voltastraße** — **U8**

18-04-1930 — **Bernauer Straße** — **U8**

U8 — Rosenthaler Platz — 18-04-1930

Der U-Bhf **Rosenthaler Platz** entspricht weitgehend dem Normaltyp der alten Linie D: relativ hohe, seitlich abgerundete Decken; Kacheln, hier in einem starken Orangeton, sowohl an den Wänden als auch an den Mittelstützen; schwarze Stationsschilder. Der Nordzugang ist in die Bebauung integriert, im südlichen Zugangsbereich wurden 2006 zwei Aufzüge eingebaut.

Bis auf die flache Decke entspricht auch der in Blau gehaltene U-Bhf **Weinmeisterstraße** dem Normaltyp der U8. Hier lagen ursprünglich die beiden östlichen Ausgänge in der Bebauung, der nordöstliche existiert nicht mehr, der südöstliche (unten) sowie ein neuer südwestlicher wurden hingegen 1990 auf den Bürgersteig gelegt.

Am **Alexanderplatz** nimmt die U8 den linken Balken des H im H-förmigen Bahnhofskomplex ein. Anders als bei der hier schon 17 Jahre früher verkehrenden U2 sind die gleichzeitig gebauten Bahnhofsteile für die U5 und U8 sehr ähnlich gestaltet. Beide wurden 2004 grundsaniert, dabei verschwand die originelle Skulptur am südlichen Bahnsteigende.

Rosenthaler Platz station generally corresponds to the standard type developed for the old line D: rather high, laterally rounded ceilings; tiles (here in a strong orange tone) both on walls and centre pillars; and black station signs. The northern access is integrated into a building, while at the southern entrance, two lifts were installed in 2006.

Except for its flat ceiling, **Weinmeisterstraße** station with its blue colour scheme also follows the standard station type of line U8. Originally, the two eastern exits were located inside buildings, but while the northeastern one no longer exists, the southeastern (left) plus a new southwestern one were placed on the pavement in 1990.

At **Alexanderplatz**, the U8 platform constitutes the left bar of the H in the H-shaped underground station. Unlike line U2, which had started running here 17 years earlier, the station parts for line U5 and U8 were built at the same time and therefore boast similar designs. Both were fully refurbished in 2004, when the unusual sculpture at the southern end of the platform disappeared.

18-04-1930 **Weinmeisterstraße** **U8**

18-04-1930 **Alexanderplatz** **U8**

S U2 U5

U8 — Jannowitzbrücke — 18-04-1930

Der U-Bhf **Jannowitzbrücke** liegt direkt nördlich der Spreequerung in eineinhalbfacher Tiefenlage. Durch die kleineren, rechteckigen Wandfliesen und unverkleideten, genieteten Stahlstützen ähnelt er eher den Bahnhöfen der Linie E (U5) als dem Standardtyp der U8. Hier konnte man bereits zwei Tage nach Öffnung der Berliner Mauer, nämlich am 11.11.1989, wieder ein- und aussteigen.

Der U-Bhf **Heinrich-Heine-Straße** war der letzte Geisterbahnhof auf Ost-Berliner Gebiet, bevor die U8 wieder den Westen erreichte. Durch die lange Schließung blieben die Stationen in einem sehr ursprünglichen Zustand erhalten. Während der nordöstliche Eingang weiterhin in ein Gebäude integriert ist, sind die anderen zwei wegen zurückversetzter Neubebauung heute freistehend, jedoch eingehaust.

Der U-Bhf **Moritzplatz** stammt nicht wie die übrigen jener Zeit von A. Grenander, sondern von Peter Behrens. Als Besonderheit fallen die mit Aluminiumleisten eingefassten Säulen auf. Die Aufgänge der als Kreuzungsbahnhof konzipierten Anlage liegen mittig und führen über ein Zwischengeschoss an alle Seiten des quadratischen Platzes.

The platform at U-Bahn station **Jannowitzbrücke** lies just north of the River Spree on level -2. The smaller, rectangular wall tiles and the uncovered, riveted steel columns make this station more like those on line E (U5) than the standard type on line U8. Service was restarted here only two days after the opening of the Berlin Wall, namely on 11th November 1989.

Heinrich-Heine-Straße was the last ghost station in East Berlin territory before line U8 returned to West Berlin. As a result of the long closure, most stations preserved their original styles. While the northeastern entrance is still integrated into a building, the other two now stand alone and are encased, as the new houses were built further back (above).

Unlike most other stations of the time, **Moritzplatz** was not designed by A. Grenander, but by Peter Behrens. A special feature are the aluminium rails which border the columns. The entrances to this station, which was laid out as a future interchange between two lines, are located on all four sides of the square and lead to a mezzanine in the middle of the station.

06-04-1928 **Heinrich-Heine-Straße** **U8**

06-04-1928 **Moritzplatz** **U8**

U8 — Kottbusser Tor — 12-02-1928

▶ U1

Farblich ähnelt der unterirdische Teil des U-Bahnhofs **Kottbusser Tor** stark der Station Heinrich-Heine-Straße mit einer etwas blassen hellvioletten Kennfarbe. Über ein mittiges Zwischengeschoss erreicht man fünf Ausgänge rund um den Platz sowie Rolltreppen zum Hochbahnhof der U1. 2005 wurde ein direkter Ausgang am nördlichen Bahnsteigende wieder geöffnet (rechts).

Weitgehend im Ursprungszustand ist der U-Bhf **Schönleinstraße** erhalten. Sonst dem Normaltyp entsprechend, fallen hier die weißen Stationsschilder sowie die sonst auf der Nordsüdbahn (U6) anzutreffenden gezackten Eingangssignete, sog. „Grenander-Portale", an den südlichen Zugängen auf. Außerdem kontrastiert der dunklere blaugrüne Farbton der Kacheln an den Säulen mit den helleren Wänden.

Die breite, jedoch niedrige Bahnsteighalle der U8 am **Hermannplatz** liegt direkt unter der Straßenoberfläche und hängt fast rechtwinkelig über der großzügigen Halle der U7. Beide Bahnhofsteile werden durch den Gelb-Grau-Kontrast der Kacheln geprägt, auch wenn die U8-Ebene im Vergleich zu jener der U7 sehr einfach gehalten ist.

The pale mauve colour scheme in the underground portion of **Kottbusser Tor** station is similar to that at Heinrich-Heine-Straße. The five exits that spread out around the square as well as the escalators that lead up to the elevated U1 platform can be reached via a central mezzanine. In 2005, a direct exit at the northern end of the platform was reopened (above).

Schönleinstraße station is preserved in almost its original state. Though it mostly corresponds to the standard type, the station features white station signs plus pointed entrance logos typical of the 'Nordsüdbahn' (U6) at the southern accesses. In addition, the darker blue-green colour of the tiles on the columns contrasts with the brighter walls.

The wide but low U8 platform hall at **Hermannplatz** lies directly below the road surface, and almost perpendicularly to the spacious hall of line U7. Both station parts are characterised by the contrast of yellow and grey tiles, although compared to the impressive U7 level, the U8 level is rather modest.

17-07-1927 | Schönleinstraße | U8

7-07-1927 | Hermannplatz | U8

U7

141

U8 Boddinstraße 17-07-1927

Der Bau des U-Bhf **Boddinstraße** erfolgte bereits 1919 bis 1921, weshalb er noch in einfacher Tiefenlage ohne Zwischengeschosse geplant worden war. Ungewöhnlich ist auch die Decke mit ihren gewölbten Abschnitten ähnlich wie bei der U6. Den südlichen Eingang ziert wie am U-Bhf Schönleinstraße ein Nordsüdbahn-Signet.

Wie der U-Bhf Boddinstraße wird auch der U-Bhf **Leinestraße** derzeit grundsaniert, wobei die ursprüngliche Verfliesung durch eine neue, jedoch weitgehend identische ausgetauscht wird. Leinestraße war 67 Jahre lang südliche Endstation der U8, auch wenn der Tunnel bereits 1929 fast bis zum S-Bahn-Südring gebaut wurde.

Der heutige Endbahnhof **Hermannstraße** wurde bereits in den späten 1920er Jahren teilweise im Rohbau errichtet und diente während des Kriegs als Luftschutzbunker. Der 1996 endlich vollendete U-Bahnhof liegt rechtwinkelig unter dem S-Bahnhof, separate Ausgänge führen beiderseits des breiten Eisenbahneinschnitts an die Oberfläche (unten). Trotz der verwendeten Glasplatten, die bereits abfallen, lehnt sich die Station gestalterisch an die älteren U8-Bahnhöfe an.

Hermannstraße

The construction of **Boddinstraße** station was already carried out between 1919 and 1921, when stations were still placed just below street level without mezzanines. Unusually, the ceiling features arched sections similar to those on line U6. Like at Schönleinstraße, the southern entrance boasts a 'Nordsüdbahn' logo.

Like Boddinstraße, **Leinestraße** station is also currently being renovated, with the original tiles being replaced by new, but almost identical ones. Leinestraße remained line U8's southern terminus for 67 years, even though the tunnel had already been built almost all the way to the S-Bahn's southern ring by 1929.

Partially built in the late 1920s, the current terminus **Hermannstraße** served as an air-raid shelter during the World War II. Finally completed in 1996, it lies perpendicularly under the S-Bahn station, with separate exits leading to the surface on either side of the wide railway cutting (left). Despite the use of glass tiles, many of which have already fallen off, the station is in the style of the older stations.

04-08-1929 **Leinestraße** U8

3-07-1996 **Hermannstraße** U8

143

U9 — Osloer Straße – Rathaus Steglitz

Zwar schon früher in verschiedenen Varianten geplant, entstand die Linie U9 Ende der 1950er Jahre als reine West-Berliner Linie, um die nördlichen Bezirke mit der City-West rund um den Bahnhof Zoo und dem Süden zu verbinden. Die Inbetriebnahme des mittleren Abschnitts der damals noch als Linie G bezeichneten Strecke erfolgte im August 1961 knapp zwei Wochen nach dem Bau der Berliner Mauer. Für die Gestaltung der U-Bahnhöfe war Bruno Grimmek verantwortlich, der in der Tradition Alfred Grenanders einen Standardtyp mit unterschiedlichen Kennfarben für die einzelnen Stationen entwarf. Dem Zeitgeist der 1950er Jahre entsprechend kamen dabei bei der Wandverfliesung Pastellfarben zur Anwendung. Die geschwungene Schmetterlingsdecke sowie die sechseckigen Mittelstützen kennzeichnen diese Epoche, die auch auf dem Tegeler Abschnitt der U6 zu bewundern ist.

Although line U9 had earlier been planned with different routes, by the late 1950s it had evolved into an exclusively West Berlin line to connect the northern districts with the 'City-West' around Zoo Station and the southern districts. The opening of the central portion of the route, then known as line G, took place in August 1961, just two weeks after the erection of the Berlin Wall. Bruno Grimmek was responsible for the design of the stations, and following the tradition of Alfred Grenander, he designed a standard type with a different colour scheme for each station. Reflecting the fashion of the 1950s, pastel colours were used on the tiled walls. The curved 'butterfly' ceilings as well as the hexagonal centre supports are characteristic of this era of construction, which is also visible on the Tegel extension of line U6.

U9

12.5 km (gänzlich unterirdisch | *completely underground*)
18 Bahnhöfe | *stations*

28-08-1961: Leopoldplatz – Spichernstraße
29-01-1971: Spichernstraße – Walther-Schreiber-Platz
30-09-1974: Walther-Schreiber-Platz – Rathaus Steglitz
30-04-1976: Leopoldplatz – Osloer Straße

Kurfürstendamm

Turmstraße

In den 1970er Jahren folgten mehrere Verlängerungen in beiden Richtungen, wobei nun Rainer G. Rümmler mehr Abwechslung in die Gestaltung der Bahnhöfe brachte, oft mit einem Bezug zum Stationsnamen oder zur Umgebung des Bahnhofs.

Nach dem Fall der Mauer im November 1989 wurden die bereits weit fortgeschrittenen Planungen für eine weitere Verlängerung von Steglitz bis Lankwitz eingestellt, da andere Projekte, vor allem der Wiederaufbau unterbrochener Verbindungen zwischen Ost und West, Vorrang hatten. Im Norden war einst eine Erweiterung bis ins Pankower Zentrum vorgesehen, wohin auch die U2 verlängert werden sollte.

Auch in der wiedervereinten Stadt gehört die U9 zu den am meisten frequentierten und schnellsten U-Bahn-Linien.

In the 1970s, the line was extended in both directions in various stages, with architect Rainer G. Rümmler now bringing more diversity into the design of the stations, often taking the station's name or surroundings as a source of inspiration.

After the fall of the Berlin Wall in November 1989, well-advanced plans for a further extension from Steglitz to Lankwitz were shelved because other projects, in particular the reconstruction of the interrupted connections between East and West, were given priority. In the north, an extension to the centre of Pankow was once planned, where line U9 would meet line U2, which was also to be extended there.

In the reunited city, line U9 has remained one of the busiest and fastest U-Bahn lines.

Intzelstraße

Erfahren Sie mehr über diese Linie in unserer Reihe:

Berliner U-Bahn-Linien: U9 – Nord-Süd durch die City-West

von Alexander Seefeldt

Planung
Bau
Betrieb
Stationen

ISBN 978-3-936573-30-5

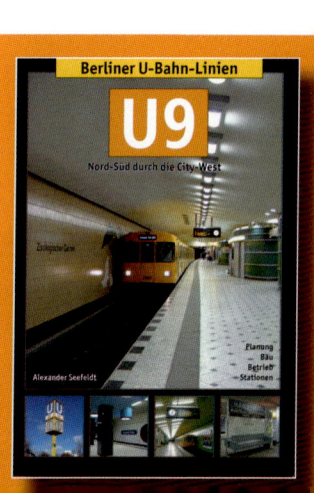

U9 Osloer Straße 30-04-1976

▶ U8

Die nördliche Endstation der U9, **Osloer Straße**, ist Teil eines Turmbahnhofs, so dass man bequem zur darunterliegenden U8 umsteigen kann. Ursprünglich waren beiden Bahnhofsteile sehr ähnlich, mit der norwegischen Flagge als Faserzementplatten an den Seitenwänden und Aluminiumpaneelen an den Bahnsteigwänden. Die Decke war hier anfangs durchgehend dunkelblau gestrichen, später weiß. 2004 wurde der gesamte U-Bahnhof modernisiert, auf dem U9-Bahnsteig wurden die Aluminiumbleche durch kräftig rote Fliesen ersetzt und die Decke nur über dem Gleisbereich blau gestrichen.

Ähnlich umgestaltet wurde der U-Bhf **Nauener Platz**, dessen Säulen ursprünglich ebenfalls eine Aluminiumblechverkleidung hatten. Auch hier war die Decke zwischenzeitlich weiß gestrichen.

Der U9-Bahnsteig auf der unteren Ebene des Turmbahnhofs **Leopoldplatz** präsentiert sich bis auf die vor einigen Jahren teilweise hellgrün gestrichene Decke weitgehend im Originalzustand. Neben der U6 kann man hier auch zur Straßenbahn umsteigen.

Osloer Straße

The northern terminus of line U9, **Osloer Straße**, is part of a bi-level station allowing convenient interchange with line U8, which stops on the lower level. Originally, the two platform levels were very similar, with the Norwegian flag depicted on fibre cement panels on the side walls, and aluminium panels on the platform walls. The ceiling on the U9 level was initially dark blue, but it was later painted white. In 2004, the entire underground complex was modernised, and for line U9, bright red tiles replaced the old aluminium panels, and the ceiling was painted blue just above the tracks.

A similar restyling was carried out at **Nauener Platz**, where the columns were originally also clad in aluminium panels. Again, for some years the ceiling used to be white.

Except for the ceiling, which was painted light green a few years ago, the lower level of the bi-level interchange station **Leopoldplatz** largely preserves its original look. Besides U6, passengers can also transfer to the tram here.

30-04-1976 — **Nauener Platz** — U9

28-08-1961 — **Leopoldplatz** — U9

U6

U9 — Amrumer Straße — 28-08-1961

Die Seitenwände im U-Bhf **Amrumer Straße** blieben jahrelang unverkleidet, nachdem die ursprünglichen weißen Fliesen abgefallen waren. 2005 wurde der Bahnhof neu gestaltet, mit türkisfarbenen Glasplatten auf einem dunkelblauen Hintergrund und mit farblich abgestimmtem Glasmosaik an den sechseckigen Stützen. Gleichzeitig wurde ein Aufzug eingebaut.

Der U-Bhf **Westhafen** wurde Ende der 1990er Jahre komplett umgestaltet und im Rahmen eines europäischen Projekts dem Thema Menschenrechte gewidmet. Während die einzelnen Artikel an den Wänden zitiert werden, haben sich alle Satzzeichen auf den gelben Mittelstützen versammelt. Ursprünglich waren die Stützen grün und die Wände gelb. Seit 2003 kommt man mit zwei Aufzügen zur S-Bahn.

Weitgehend im Original ist der U-Bhf **Birkenstraße** erhalten, dessen Hellgrün an Wänden und Säulen einen Zusammenhang zum Stationsnamen vermuten lässt, selbst die Steine am Bahnsteigende und an den mittig angeordneten Treppen erinnern an Birkenrinde.

Westhafen

For many years, the side walls at **Amrumer Straße** remained uncovered after the original white tiles had fallen off. Finally in 2005, the station was refurbished with turquoise glass panels mounted on a dark blue background, and a matching glass mosaic on the hexagonal columns. At the same time, a lift was installed.

Westhafen station was completely restyled in the late 1990s as part of a European project dedicated to Human Rights. While the convention articles are quoted on the walls (above), all the punctuation marks are collected on the yellow centre pillars. Originally, the pillars were green and the walls yellow. Since 2003, two lifts have provided a stepfree link to the S-Bahn.

Birkenstraße station has hardly been modified: the light green tiles on the walls and pillars hint at the colour of the leaves of the tree, from which the station takes its name. Even the stones used on the walls at the end of the platform and the centrally positioned staircases are reminiscent of birch bark.

28-08-1961 | Westhafen | U9

28-08-1961 | Birkenstraße | U9

149

U9 — Turmstraße — 28-08-1961

Der U-Bhf **Turmstraße** gehört zum Standardtyp der ursprünglichen U9, jedoch findet man hier neben den Ausgängen an den Bahnsteigenden auch einen mittigen Aufgang, der als Übergang zur U5 konzipiert war. Um diesen stark frequentierten U-Bahnhof etwas aufzuwerten, wurden die sechseckigen Stützen 2010/11 mit verschiedenen Motiven aus der Umgebung verziert.

Ebenfalls dem Standardtyp entspricht der U-Bhf **Hansaplatz**, allerdings weisen seine Seitenwände eine kleinteilige, graue Wandverfliesung auf. Außerdem verfügt er über keine Zwischengeschosse, stattdessen münden die jeweiligen Ausgänge in oberirdische Pavillons (unten). Das ursprüngliche Bahnsteigmobiliar ist weitgehend erhalten.

Der stark frequentierte U-Bhf **Zoologischer Garten** wurde in den letzten 50 Jahren mehrmals umgestaltet. Die bräunliche Wandverfliesung mit Tiermotiven ersetzte 1987 zur 750-Jahr-Feier Berlins die originalen orangefarbenen Fliesen, der Granitboden und die grüne Glasverkleidung der Säulen und Läden folgte erst 2002-2005.

Turmstraße station is of the standard type developed for the original U9, although besides the exits at the platform ends, there is a central staircase designed for a future interchange with line U5. To upgrade this busy station a little, the hexagonal columns were decorated in 2010/11 with various motifs from the surrounding area.

Hansaplatz station also corresponds to the standard type, although its side walls are clad in small grey tiles. It is also different in that it has no mezzanines, but instead features surface entrance pavilions (left). Most of the original platform furniture has been preserved.

The much-used **Zoologischer Garten** station has been refurbished several times in its 50-year history. The original orange tiles were replaced with brown tiles with animal motifs for Berlin's 750th anniversary in 1987, while the granite floor and the green glass that covers the pillars and shops only followed between 2002 and 2005.

Hansaplatz

Hansaplatz — U9
28-08-1961

Zoologischer Garten — U9
28-08-1961

U9 — Kurfürstendamm

28-08-1961

▶ U1

Die Wände im U-Bhf **Kurfürstendamm** wurden wie im U-Bhf Zoologischer Garten auch 1987 neu verkleidet, jedoch verwendete man dafür weitgehend dem Original gleichende Fliesen. Vom nördlichen Bahnsteigende gelangt man mit einem Aufzug nur zur U1 Richtung Uhlandstraße und von dort an die Oberfläche.

Die ersten 10 Jahre war **Spichernstraße** der südliche Endpunkt der U9. Bereits Anfang der 1990er Jahre wurden die ursprünglich blauen Wandfliesen durch weiße ersetzt und wie im U-Bhf Paradestraße durch eine farbige Komposition von Gabriele Stirl ergänzt. Leider ist der zwar typische, aber doch etwas unattraktive Asphaltboden noch vorhanden.

Der U-Bhf **Güntzelstraße** lehnt sich gestalterisch an die südliche U6 an, die wenige Jahre zuvor fertiggestellt wurde. Der Farbkontrast an Säulen und Wänden ist in umgekehrter Form in den Zwischengeschossen zu finden (siehe Seite 145).

Kurfürstendamm

Like Zoologischer Garten, the walls in **Kurfürstendamm** station were also modernised in 1987, but using tiles very similar to the original ones. The lift at the northern end of the platform only takes one to the westbound platform of line U1 (direction Uhlandstraße), but from there another one leads to the surface.

For the first 10 years, **Spichernstraße** was line U9's southern terminus. Already in the early 1990s, the original blue tiles were replaced with white ones, enhanced with a colour composition by Gabriele Stirl similar to that at Paradestraße on line U6. Unfortunately, the typical, though somewhat unattractive asphalt floor is still present.

Güntzelstraße station is similar to the stations on line U6's southern extension, which was completed a few years earlier. The same colour contrast between the columns and walls can also be found in the mezzanines, but in an inverted scheme (see p. 145).

28-08-1961 **Spichernstraße** **U9**

29-01-1971 **Güntzelstraße** **U9**

153

U9 — Berliner Straße — 29-01-1971

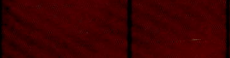

▶ U7

Die Seitenwände in der oberen Ebene des Turmbahnhofs **Berliner Straße** waren ursprünglich mit dunkelroten Fliesen verkleidet. Diese wurden 2000/2001 durch rote Emailplatten ersetzt, während die Wände auf den Bahnsteigen weiße Fliesen erhielten. Gleichzeitig wurden Aufzüge eingebaut. Zwischen den beiden U9-Bahnsteigen, die nur am nördlichen Ende miteinander verbunden sind, liegt ein Autotunnel.

Als einzige Station auf der U9 hat der U-Bhf **Bundesplatz** Seitenbahnsteige, was einerseits durch einen weiteren Autotunnel entlang der Bundesallee, andererseits durch den Übergang zur S-Bahn bedingt war. Die Hintergleiswände waren ursprünglich in beiden Bahnsteigbereichen blau und die Bahnsteigwände weiß gefliest. 2008/09 wurde der Bahnhof saniert, die Hintergleiswände bekamen Emailplatten (Richtung Steglitz blau, Richtung Osloer Straße braun), während die Bahnsteigwände farblich entsprechend neu verfliest wurden.

Der U-Bhf **Friedrich-Wilhelm-Platz** präsentiert sich bis auf die leicht veränderten Leuchtkörper weitgehend im Zustand der 1970er Jahre, auch wenn an mehreren Stellen die Fliesen abgefallen sind.

The side walls on the upper level of the bi-level **Berliner Straße** station were originally covered with dark red tiles, which were replaced with red enamelled panels in 2000/2001, while the walls on the platforms were clad with white tiles. At the same time, lifts were installed. A road tunnel lies between the two U9 platforms, which are only connected at the northern end.

The only station on line U9 with side platforms is **Bundesplatz**, due to another road tunnel along Bundesallee and also due to the interchange with the S-Bahn. Originally, the side walls in both station areas had blue tiles and the platform walls white ones. In 2008/09, the station was restyled, with the inner walls being clad with enamelled panels (blue for the southbound platform, brown for the northbound), while the platform walls were tiled accordingly.

Besides the slightly modified lamps, Friedrich-Wilhelm-Platz station largely preserves its 1970s appearance, although the tiles have started falling off in several places.

Bundesplatz — U9
29-01-1971

Friedrich-Wilhelm-Platz — U9
29-01-1971

U9 Walther-Schreiber-Platz
29-01-1971

Mit seinen blauen Faserzementplatten an den Hintergleiswänden ähnelt der U-Bhf **Walther-Schreiber-Platz** einigen zeitgleich entstandenen Stationen auf der U7 auf ihrem Weg durch Schöneberg. Die gewölbte Decke wiederum lehnt sich an die ‚preußischen Kappen' von Berlins ältesten U-Bahnhöfen an. Seit 2009 ist die Station auch per Aufzug zugänglich.

Den doppelstöckigen U-Bhf **Schloßstraße**, der als bequeme Umsteigestation für die U9 und die U10 ausgelegt war, entwarf nicht der damalige Hausarchitekt Rainer G. Rümmler, sondern das Architektenpaar Ralf Schüler und Ursulina Schüler-Witte. Dabei herrscht Sichtbeton ergänzt mit Plastikverkleidungen vor. Die jeweils ungenutzte Bahnsteigseite ist seit 2003 durch einen Gitterzaun abgetrennt.

Der heutige Endbahnhof **Rathaus Steglitz** war eigentlich für die U10 gedacht, der Rohbau des für die U9 vorgesehenen Bahnhofsteils verbirgt sich auf der Zwischenebene hinter provisorischen Wänden. Der nördliche Zugangsbereich wurde als Übergang zum Einkaufszentrum ‚Das Schloss' 2006 sehr nobel umgestaltet (unten).

Schloßstraße

With its blue fibre cement panels on the walls, **Walther-Schreiber-Platz** station resembles some of the U7 stations on its Schöneberg section, which were built at the same time. The vaulted ceiling, however, is reminiscent of the so-called 'Prussian caps' typical of Berlin's oldest U-Bahn stations. Since 2009, the station has been fully accessible via two lifts.

The bi-level **Schloßstraße** station was not designed by former in-house architect Rainer G. Rümmler, but by the architects Ralf Schüler and Ursulina Schüler-Witte. It is characterised by exposed concrete enhanced with plastic elements. The station was laid out for cross-platform interchange between lines U9 and U10; the two unused platform edges have been fenced off since 2003.

The platform of today's terminus **Rathaus Steglitz** was also intended for line U10, while the unfinished platform actually laid out for line U9 lies hidden on the mezzanine level behind makeshift walls. The northern entrance area was restyled in 2006 as it functions as a direct access to the shopping centre 'Das Schloss' (left).

Rathaus Steglitz

30-09-1974 — Schloßstraße — U9

30-09-1974 — Rathaus Steglitz — U9

Bahnhofsverzeichnis

BEISPIEL | *EXAMPLE*

Aktueller Name | *Current name* — Linie | *Line* — Eröffnungsdatum | *Opening date* — Seite mit Bild | *Page with photo* — Seite mit Bild und Text | *Page with photo & text*

Eberswalder Straße U2 01-07-1913 ▶ *(17)·35*
[1913 > Danziger Straße; 1950-1991 > Dimitroffstraße]

Frühere Namen | *Previous names*

Aktuelle Zusatznamen (in Klammern angeführt) werden in der Regel auf offiziellen Netzplänen und bei akustischen Ansagen weggelassen.
Current name appendages (shown in brackets) are generally omitted on official system maps and acoustic announcements.

Adenauerplatz U7 28-04-1978 ▶ *(96)·108*
Afrikanische Straße (Friedrich-Ebert-Siedlung) U6 03-05-1956 ▶ *80*
Alexanderplatz U2 01-07-1913 ▶ *33*
Alexanderplatz U5 21-12-1930 ▶ *(55)·60*
Alexanderplatz U8 18-04-1930 ▶ *137*
Alt-Mariendorf U6 28-02-1966 ▶ *95*
Alt-Tegel U6 31-05-1958 ▶ *76*
[1958-1992 > Tegel]
Alt-Tempelhof U6 28-02-1966 ▶ *93*
Altstadt Spandau U7 01-10-1984 ▶ *99*
Amrumer Straße U9 28-08-1961 ▶ *148*
[1961-1988 > Amrumer Str. (Rudolf-Virchow-Krankenhaus)]
Augsburger Straße U3 08-05-1961 ▶ *48*
Bayerischer Platz U4 01-12-1910 ▶ *52*
Bayerischer Platz U7 29-01-1971 ▶ *(96)·111*
Berliner Rathaus U5 ~2019 ▶ *59*
Berliner Straße U7 29-01-1971 ▶ *(97)·111*
Berliner Straße U9 29-01-1971 ▶ *154*
Bernauer Straße U8 18-04-1930 ▶ *135*
Biesdorf-Süd U5 01-07-1988 ▶ *68*
Birkenstraße U9 28-08-1961 ▶ *149*
Bismarckstraße U2 28-04-1978 ▶ *22*
Bismarckstraße U7 28-04-1978 ▶ *107*
Blaschkoallee U7 28-09-1963 ▶ *121*
Blissestraße U7 29-01-1971 ▶ *110*
Boddinstraße U8 17-07-1927 ▶ *142*
Borsigwerke U6 31-05-1958 ▶ *77*
Brandenburger Tor U5 08-08-2009 ▶ *57*
Breitenbachplatz U3 12-10-1913 ▶ *44*
Britz-Süd U7 28-09-1963 ▶ *123*
Bülowstraße U2 11-03-1902 ▶ *27*
Bundesplatz U9 29-01-1971 ▶ *155*
Bundestag U5 08-08-2009 ▶ *(55)·57*
Cottbusser Platz U5 01-07-1989 ▶ *71*
Dahlem-Dorf U3 12-10-1913 ▶ *(39)·43*
Deutsche Oper U2 14-05-1906 ▶ *23*
[1906 > Bismarckstraße; 1929 > Städtische Oper (Bismarckstr.);
1934 > Deutsches Opernhaus; 1961-1978 > Deutsche Oper (Bismarckstr.)]
Eberswalder Straße U2 01-07-1913 ▶ *(17)·35*
[1913 > Danziger Straße; 1950-1991 > Dimitroffstraße]
Eisenacher Straße U7 29-01-1971 ▶ *112*
Elsterwerdaer Platz U5 01-07-1988 ▶ *69*
Ernst-Reuter-Platz U2 14-12-1902 ▶ *23*
[1902-1953 > Knie]
Fehrbelliner Platz U3 12-10-1913 ▶ *(38)·46*
Fehrbelliner Platz U7 29-01-1971 ▶ *(97)·108*
Frankfurter Allee U5 21-12-1930 ▶ *65*
[1930 > Frankfurter Allee; 1937 > Frankfurter Allee (Ringbahn);
1949-1961 > Stalinallee (Ringbahn)]
Frankfurter Tor U5 21-12-1930 ▶ *63*
[1930 > Petersburger Straße; 1946 > Bersarinstraße; 01/1958 > Bersarinstraße (Frankfurter Tor); 06/1958 > Frankfurter Tor; 1991 >
Rathaus Friedrichshain; 1996-1998 > Petersburger Straße]
Franz-Neumann-Platz (Am Schäfersee) U8 27-04-1987 ▶ *132*
Französische Straße U6 30-01-1923 ▶ *(75)·87*
Friedrich-Wilhelm-Platz U9 29-01-1971 ▶ *155*
Friedrichsfelde U5 21-12-1930 ▶ *67*
[1958-1970 > Friedrichsfelde (Tierpark)]
Friedrichstraße U6 30-01-1923 ▶ *(74)·86*
[1923 > Bahnhof Friedrichstraße; 1924 > Stadtbahn (Friedrichstr.);
1936-1976 > Bahnhof Friedrichstraße]
Gesundbrunnen U8 18-04-1930 ▶ *(126)·134*
Gleisdreieck U1 03-11-1912 ▶ *11*
Gleisdreieck U2 03-11-1912 ▶ *27*
Gneisenaustraße U7 19-04-1924 ▶ *115*

Görlitzer Bahnhof U1 18-02-1902 ▶ *14*
[1902 > Oranienstraße; 1926-1982 > Görlitzer Bahnhof (Oranienstraße)]
Grenzallee U7 21-12-1930 ▶ *120*
Güntzelstraße U9 29-01-1971 ▶ *(145)·153*
Halemweg U7 01-10-1980 ▶ *(97)·103*
Hallesches Tor U1 18-02-1902 ▶ *(7)·12*
Hallesches Tor U6 30-01-1923 ▶ *89*
Hansaplatz U9 28-08-1961 ▶ *151*
Haselhorst U7 01-10-1984 ▶ *100*
Hauptbahnhof U5 08-08-2009 ▶ *56*
Hausvogteiplatz U2 01-10-1908 ▶ *31*
Heidelberger Platz U3 12-10-1913 ▶ *(39)·45*
Heinrich-Heine-Straße U8 06-04-1928 ▶ *139*
[1928-1960 > Neanderstraße]
Hellersdorf U5 01-07-1989 ▶ *72*
Hermannplatz U7 11-04-1926 ▶ *117*
Hermannplatz U8 17-07-1927 ▶ *141*
Hermannstraße U8 13-07-1996 ▶ *143*
Hohenzollernplatz U3 12-10-1913 ▶ *47*
Holzhauser Straße U6 31-05-1958 ▶ *77*
Hönow U5 01-07-1989 ▶ *73*
Innsbrucker Platz U4 01-12-1910 ▶ *53*
[1910-1933 > Hauptstraße]
Jakob-Kaiser-Platz U7 01-10-1980 ▶ *104*
Jannowitzbrücke U8 18-04-1930 ▶ *138*
Johannisthaler Chaussee (Gropiusstadt) U7 02-01-1970 ▶ *123*
[1970-1972 > Johannisthaler Chaussee]
Jungfernheide U7 01-10-1980 ▶ *105*
Kaiserdamm U2 29-03-1908 ▶ *21*
[1908 > Kaiserdamm; 1936 > Kaiserdamm (Messedamm);
1967 > Adenauerdamm; 1968 > Kaiserdamm]
Kaiserin-Augusta-Straße U6 28-02-1966 ▶ *93*
Karl-Bonhoeffer-Nervenklinik U8 24-09-1994 ▶ *129*
Karl-Marx-Straße U7 11-04-1926 ▶ *119*
[1926-1946 > Bergstraße]
Kaulsdorf-Nord U5 01-07-1989 ▶ *70*
[1989-1991 > Albert-Norden-Straße]
Kleistpark U7 29-01-1971 ▶ *113*
Klosterstraße U2 01-07-1913 ▶ *(17)·33*
Kochstraße (Checkpoint Charlie) U6 30-01-1923 ▶ *(74)·89*
[1923-1995 > Kochstraße]
Konstanzer Straße U7 28-04-1978 ▶ *108*
Kottbusser Tor U1 18-02-1902 ▶ *13*
Kottbusser Tor U8 12-02-1928 ▶ *140*
Krumme Lanke U3 22-12-1929 ▶ *40*
Kurfürstendamm U1 02-09-1961 ▶ *8*
Kurfürstendamm U9 28-08-1961 ▶ *(144)·152*
Kurfürstenstraße U1 24-10-1926 ▶ *10*
Kurt-Schumacher-Platz U6 03-05-1956 ▶ *79*
Leinestraße U8 04-08-1929 ▶ *143*
Leopoldplatz U6 08-03-1923 ▶ *82*
Leopoldplatz U9 28-08-1961 ▶ *147*
Lichtenberg U5 21-12-1930 ▶ *(54)·66*
[1930 > Lichtenberg (Zentralfriedhof); 1935 > Bahnhof Lichtenberg
(Zentralfriedhof); 1965-1974 > Bahnhof Lichtenberg]
Lindauer Allee U8 24-09-1994 ▶ *(127)·130*
Lipschitzallee U7 02-01-1970 ▶ *123*
Louis-Lewin-Straße U5 01-07-1989 ▶ *73*
[1989-1991 > Paul-Verner-Straße]
Magdalenenstraße U5 21-12-1930 ▶ *65*
Märkisches Museum U2 01-07-1913 ▶ *32*
[1913-1935 > Inselbrücke]
Mehringdamm U6 19-04-1924 ▶ *90*
[1924 > Belle-Alliance-Straße; 1946-1947 > Franz-Mehring-Straße]
Mehringdamm U7 19-04-1924 ▶ *115*

Station Index

Mendelssohn-Bartholdy-Park U2 01-10-1998 ▶ *28*
Mierendorffplatz U7 01-10-1980 ▶ *105*
Möckernbrücke U1 18-02-1902 ▶ *11*
Möckernbrücke U7 28-02-1966 ▶ *114*
Mohrenstraße U2 01-10-1908 ▶ *29*
[1908 > Kaiserhof; 1950 > Thälmannplatz; 1986 > Otto-Grotewohl-Straße; 1991 > Mohrenstraße]
Moritzplatz U8 06-04-1928 ▶ *139*
Museumsinsel U5 ~2019 ▶ *59*
Naturkundemuseum U6 30-01-1923 ▶ *85*
[1923 > Stettiner Bahnhof; 1951 > Nordbahnhof; 1991-2009 > Zinnowitzer Straße]
Nauener Platz U9 30-04-1976 ▶ *147*
Neu-Westend U2 20-05-1922 ▶ *19*
Neue Grottkauer Straße U5 01-07-1989 ▶ *71*
[1989 > Heinz-Hoffmann-Straße; 1991-1996 > Grottkauer Str.]
Neukölln (Südring) U7 21-12-1930 ▶ *119*
[1962-1992 > Neukölln]
Nollendorfplatz U1 24-10-1926 ▶ *9*
Nollendorfplatz U2 11-03-1902 ▶ *26*
Nollendorfplatz U3 24-10-1926 ▶ *49*
Nollendorfplatz U4 01-12-1910 ▶ *51*
Nürnberger Platz (1913-1959) ▶ *48*
Olympia-Stadion U2 08-06-1913 ▶ *19*
[1913 > Stadion; 1935 > Reichssportfeld; 1950 > Olympia-Stadion; 1992-1999 > Olympia-Stadion (Ost)]
Onkel Toms Hütte U3 22-12-1929 ▶ *41*
Oranienburger Tor U6 30-01-1923 ▶ *85*
Oskar-Helene-Heim U3 22-12-1929 ▶ *(38)·41*
Osloer Straße U8 05-10-1977 ▶ *133*
Osloer Straße U9 30-04-1976 ▶ *146*
Osthafen (1902-1945) ▶ *14*
[1902-1924 > Stralauer Thor]
Otisstraße U6 31-05-1958 ▶ *78*
[1958 > Seidelstraße; 1961 > Seidelstraße (Flughafen Tegel); 1974-2003 > Seidelstraße]
Pankow U2 16-09-2000 ▶ *37*
Pankstraße U8 05-10-1977 ▶ *133*
Paracelsus-Bad U8 27-04-1987 ▶ *(126)·131*
Paradestraße U6 10-09-1927 ▶ *91*
[1927-1937 > Flughafen]
Parchimer Allee U7 28-09-1963 ▶ *121*
Paulsternstraße U7 01-10-1984 ▶ *101*
Platz der Luftbrücke U6 14-02-1926 ▶ *91*
[1926 > Kreuzberg; 1937-1975 > Flughafen]
Podbielskiallee U3 12-10-1913 ▶ *(39)·43*
Potsdamer Platz U2 18-02-1902 ▶ *29*
[1902 > Potsdamer Platz; 1907-1923 > Leipziger Platz]
Prinzenstraße U1 18-02-1902 ▶ *13*
Rathaus Neukölln U7 11-04-1926 ▶ *118*
Rathaus Reinickendorf U8 24-09-1994 ▶ *129*
Rathaus Schöneberg U4 01-12-1910 ▶ *(50)·53*
[1910-1951 > Stadtpark]
Rathaus Spandau U7 01-10-1984 ▶ *(96)·98*
Rathaus Steglitz U9 30-09-1974 ▶ *(144)·157*
Rehberge U6 03-05-1956 ▶ *81*
Reinickendorfer Straße U6 08-03-1923 ▶ *83*
Residenzstraße U8 27-04-1987 ▶ *131*
Richard-Wagner-Platz (1906-1970) ▶ *106*
[1906-1935 > Wilhelmplatz]
Richard-Wagner-Platz U7 28-04-1978 ▶ *106*
Rohrdamm U7 01-10-1980 ▶ *102*
Rosa-Luxemburg-Platz U2 01-07-1913 ▶ *34*
[1913 > Schönhauser Tor; 1934 > Horst-Wessel-Platz; 1945 > Schönhauser Tor; 1950-1978 > Luxemburgplatz]
Rosenthaler Platz U8 18-04-1930 ▶ *(126)·136*
Rüdesheimer Platz U3 12-10-1913 ▶ *45*
Rudow U7 01-07-1972 ▶ *125*
Ruhleben U2 22-12-1929 ▶ *(17)·18*

Samariterstraße U5 21-12-1930 ▶ *64*
Scharnweberstraße U6 31-05-1958 ▶ *(75)·79*
Schillingstraße U5 21-12-1930 ▶ *61*
Schlesisches Tor U1 18-02-1902 ▶ *15*
Schloßstraße U9 30-09-1974 ▶ *157*
Schönhauser Allee U2 01-07-1913 ▶ *36*
[1913-1936 > Bahnhof Nordring]
Schönleinstraße U8 17-07-1927 ▶ *141*
[1951-1992 > Kottbusser Damm (Schönleinstraße)]
Schwartzkopffstraße U6 08-03-1923 ▶ *84*
[1923 > Schwartzkopffstr.; 1951 > Walter-Ulbricht-Stadion; 1973-1991 > Stadion der Weltjugend]
Seestraße U6 08-03-1923 ▶ *81*
Senefelderplatz U2 01-07-1913 ▶ *35*
Siemensdamm U7 01-10-1980 ▶ *103*
Sophie-Charlotte-Platz U2 29-03-1908 ▶ *(16)·21*
Spichernstraße U3 02-06-1959 ▶ *47*
Spichernstraße U9 28-08-1961 ▶ *153*
Spittelmarkt U2 01-10-1908 ▶ *31*
Stadtmitte U2 01-10-1908 ▶ *30*
[1908 > Friedrichstraße; 1923 > Leipziger Straße (Mohrenstr.); 1924 > Friedrichstadt (Mohrenstr.); 1936-~1970 > Stadtmitte (Mohrenstr.)]
Stadtmitte U6 30-01-1923 ▶ *88*
[1923 > Leipziger Straße; 1924 > Friedrichstadt (Leipziger Str.); 1936-1992 > Stadtmitte (Leipziger Str.)]
Strausberger Platz U5 21-12-1930 ▶ *62*
Südstern U7 14-12-1924 ▶ *116*
[1924 > Hasenheide; 1933 > Kaiser-Friedrich-Platz; 1939-1947 > Gardepionierplatz]
Tempelhof (Südring) U6 22-12-1929 ▶ *92*
[1962-1992 > Tempelhof]
Theodor-Heuss-Platz U2 29-03-1908 ▶ *(16)·20*
[1908 > Reichskanzlerplatz; 1933 > Adolf-Hitler-Platz; 1945 > Reichskanzlerplatz; 1963 > Theodor-Heuss-Platz]
Thielplatz U3 12-10-1913 ▶ *42*
Tierpark U5 25-06-1973 ▶ *67*
Turmstraße U9 28-08-1961 ▶ *(145)·150*
Uhlandstraße U1 12-10-1913 ▶ *7*
[1949-1961 > Uhlandstraße (Kurfürstendamm)]
Ullsteinstraße U6 28-02-1966 ▶ *94*
Unter den Linden U5 ~2019 ▶ *58*
Unter den Linden U6 ~2019 ▶ *58*
Viktoria-Luise-Platz U4 01-12-1910 ▶ *51*
[1910-~1920 > Viktoria-Luisen-Platz]
Vinetastraße U2 29-06-1930 ▶ *37*
[1930-1993 > Panow (Vinetastraße)]
Voltastraße U8 18-04-1930 ▶ *135*
Walther-Schreiber-Platz U9 29-01-1971 ▶ *156*
Warschauer Straße U1 17-08-1902 ▶ *(6)·15*
[1902-1995 > Warschauer Brücke]
Weberwiese U5 21-12-1930 ▶ *63*
[1930 > Memeler Straße; 1950-1991 > Marchlewskistraße]
Wedding U6 08-03-1923 ▶ *83*
[1923-1972 > Bahnhof Wedding]
Weinmeisterstraße U8 18-04-1930 ▶ *137*
Westhafen U9 28-08-1961 ▶ *149*
[1961-1992 > Putlitzstraße]
Westphalweg U6 28-02-1966 ▶ *95*
Wilmersdorfer Straße U7 28-04-1978 ▶ *107*
Wittenau (Wilhelmsruher Damm) U8 24-09-1994 ▶ *(127)·128*
Wittenbergplatz U1 12-10-1913 ▶ *9*
Wittenbergplatz U2 11-03-1902 ▶ *25*
Wittenbergplatz U3 12-10-1913 ▶ *49*
Wuhletal U5 01-07-1989 ▶ *69*
Wutzkyallee U7 02-01-1970 ▶ *124*
Yorckstraße U7 29-01-1971 ▶ *113*
Zitadelle U7 01-10-1984 ▶ *99*
Zoologischer Garten U2 11-03-1902 ▶ *24*
Zoologischer Garten U9 28-08-1961 ▶ *151*
Zwickauer Damm U7 02-01-1970 ▶ *125*

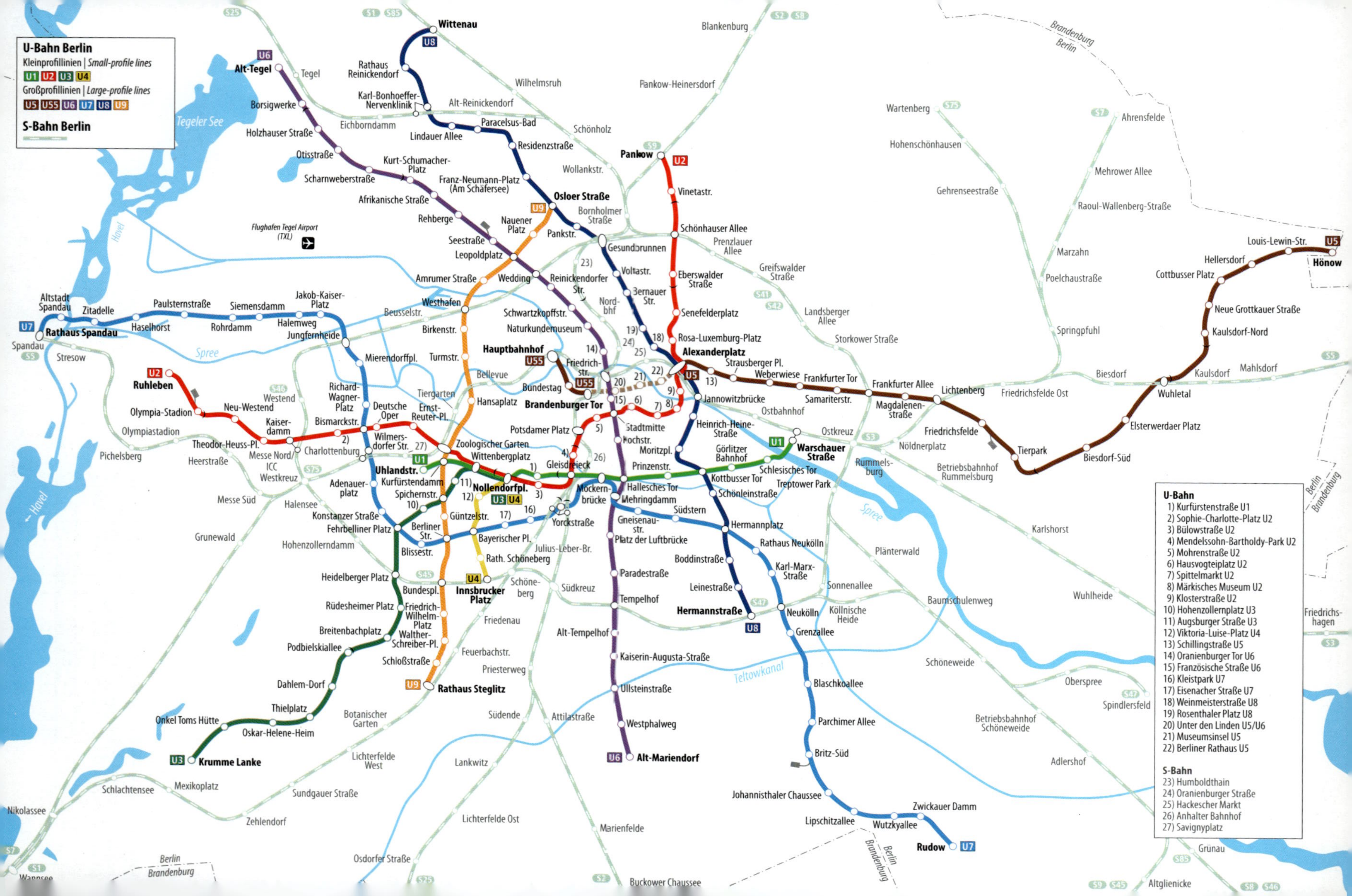

U-Bahn Berlin
Kleinprofillinien | Small-profile lines
U1 U2 U3 U4
Großprofillinien | Large-profile lines
U5 U55 U6 U7 U8 U9
S-Bahn Berlin
U-Bahn
1) Kurfürstenstraße U1
2) Sophie-Charlotte-Platz U2
3) Bülowstraße U2
4) Mendelssohn-Bartholdy-Park U2
5) Mohrenstraße U2
6) Hausvogteiplatz U2
7) Spittelmarkt U2
8) Märkisches Museum U2
9) Klosterstraße U2
10) Hohenzollernplatz U3
11) Augsburger Straße U3
12) Viktoria-Luise-Platz U4
13) Schillingstraße U5
14) Oranienburger Tor U6
15) Französische Straße U6
16) Kleistpark U7
17) Eisenacher Straße U7
18) Weinmeisterstraße U8
19) Rosenthaler Platz U8
20) Unter den Linden U5/U6
21) Museumsinsel U5
22) Berliner Rathaus U5
S-Bahn
23) Humboldthain
24) Oranienburger Straße
25) Hackescher Markt
26) Anhalter Bahnhof
27) Savignyplatz
Wittenau
Rathaus Reinickendorf
Karl-Bonhoeffer-Nervenklinik
Alt-Reinickendorf
Lindauer Allee
Paracelsus-Bad
Residenzstraße
Franz-Neumann-Platz (Am Schäfersee)
Osloer Straße
Pankstr.
Gesundbrunnen
Voltastr.
Bernauer Str.
Alt-Tegel
Borsigwerke
Holzhauser Straße
Otisstraße
Scharnweberstraße
Kurt-Schumacher-Platz
Afrikanische Straße
Rehberge
Seestraße
Leopoldplatz
Wedding
Reinickendorfer Str.
Schwartzkopffstr.
Naturkundemuseum
Friedrichstr.
Stadtmitte
Kochstr.
Hallesches Tor
Mehringdamm
Platz der Luftbrücke
Paradestraße
Tempelhof
Alt-Tempelhof
Kaiserin-Augusta-Straße
Ullsteinstraße
Westphalweg
Alt-Mariendorf
Pankow
Vinetastr.
Schönhauser Allee
Eberswalder Straße
Senefelderplatz
Rosa-Luxemburg-Platz
Alexanderplatz
Potsdamer Platz
Gleisdreieck
Nollendorfpl.
Wittenbergplatz
Zoologischer Garten
Ernst-Reuter-Pl.
Deutsche Oper
Bismarckstr.
Wilmersdorfer Str.
Kaiserdamm
Theodor-Heuss-Pl.
Neu-Westend
Olympia-Stadion
Ruhleben
Hönow
Louis-Lewin-Str.
Hellersdorf
Cottbusser Platz
Neue Grottkauer Straße
Kaulsdorf-Nord
Wuhletal
Elsterwerdaer Platz
Biesdorf-Süd
Tierpark
Friedrichsfelde
Lichtenberg
Magdalenenstraße
Frankfurter Allee
Samariterstr.
Frankfurter Tor
Weberwiese
Strausberger Pl.
Hauptbahnhof
Bundestag
Brandenburger Tor
Rathaus Spandau
Altstadt Spandau
Zitadelle
Haselhorst
Paulsternstraße
Rohrdamm
Siemensdamm
Halemweg
Jakob-Kaiser-Platz
Jungfernheide
Mierendorffpl.
Richard-Wagner-Platz
Konstanzer Straße
Fehrbelliner Platz
Blissestr.
Berliner Str.
Bayerischer Pl.
Yorckstraße
Möckernbrücke
Gneisenaustr.
Südstern
Hermannplatz
Rathaus Neukölln
Karl-Marx-Straße
Neukölln
Grenzallee
Blaschkoallee
Parchimer Allee
Britz-Süd
Johannisthaler Chaussee
Lipschitzallee
Wutzkyallee
Zwickauer Damm
Rudow
Uhlandstr.
Kurfürstendamm
Prinzenstr.
Kottbusser Tor
Görlitzer Bahnhof
Schlesisches Tor
Warschauer Straße
Jannowitzbrücke
Heinrich-Heine-Straße
Moritzpl.
Schönleinstraße
Boddinstraße
Leinestraße
Hermannstraße
Nauener Platz
Amrumer Straße
Westhafen
Birkenstr.
Turmstr.
Hansaplatz
Spichernstr.
Güntzelstr.
Bundespl.
Friedrich-Wilhelm-Platz
Walther-Schreiber-Pl.
Schloßstraße
Rathaus Steglitz
Rath. Schöneberg
Innsbrucker Platz
Adenauerplatz
Heidelberger Platz
Rüdesheimer Platz
Breitenbachplatz
Podbielskiallee
Dahlem-Dorf
Thielplatz
Oskar-Helene-Heim
Onkel Toms Hütte
Krumme Lanke
Flughafen Tegel Airport (TXL)
Tegeler See
Havel
Spree
Teltowkanal
Berlin
Brandenburg